West Sussex Library Service

WITHDRAWN

For Sale

GW00585709

200732665

THE
KINGMAKER'S
SISTERS

THE
KINGMAKER'S
SISTERS

SIX
POWERFUL
WOMEN
IN THE
WARS OF
THE ROSES

DAVID BALDWIN

The
History
Press

WEST SUSSEX COUNTY LIBRARY SERVICE	
200732665	
Askews	07-Jul-2009
942.04	

First published 2009

The History Press
The Mill, Brimscombe Port
Stroud, Gloucestershire, GL5 2QG
www.thehistorypress.co.uk

© David Baldwin, 2009

The right of David Baldwin to be identified as the Author
of this work has been asserted in accordance with the
Copyrights, Designs and Patents Act 1988.

All rights reserved. No part of this book may be reprinted
or reproduced or utilised in any form or by any electronic,
mechanical or other means, now known or hereafter invented,
including photocopying and recording, or in any information
storage or retrieval system, without the permission in writing
from the Publishers.

British Library Cataloguing in Publication Data.
A catalogue record for this book is available from the British Library.

ISBN 978 0 7509 5076 3

Typesetting and origination by The History Press
Printed in Great Britain

Contents

ILLUSTRATIONS

9   Cawood Castle Gatehouse, Yorkshire, part of the palace of the archbishops of York where Warwick, his sisters, and many members of the nobility attended the banquet held to celebrate George Neville's enthronement in September, 1465 (author)

10   Thomas, Lord Stanley, Eleanor Neville, and two others, effigies in Ormskirk Church, Lancashire, drawn by William Dugdale in 1664 (author)

11   The 'Hastings Tower' at Ashby de la Zouch Castle, Leicestershire, home of William, Lord Hastings and Katherine Neville (author)

12   The west tower of Kirby Muxloe Castle, Leicestershire, where Katherine may have spent part of her widowhood (author)

13   Ravensworth Castle, Yorkshire. The early fourteenth-century tower gatehouse and adjoining archway, home of Henry, Lord Fitzhugh and Alice Neville (author)

14   The Marmion Tower. The fifteenth-century gateway tower at West Tanfield, Yorkshire, where Alice Neville spent part of her widowhood and from where she wrote to the mayor, aldermen and council of York (author)

15   John de Vere, Earl of Oxford and Margaret Neville, re-drawn from Daniel King's original 1653 illustration of their tomb effigies in Colne Priory Church, Essex, destroyed *c.*1730 (Geoffrey Wheeler)

16   Castle Hedingham, Essex. John de Vere's bridge over the now dry moat (www.castleuk.net)

17   Signature of Richard Neville, Earl of Warwick (from Fenn's *Original Letters Written during the Reigns of Henry VI, Edward IV and Richard III*, 1787, vol. 2)

18   Signature of Eleanor Neville, Lady Stanley (John Rylands University Library, Arley Charter 30/2, re-drawn by Geoffrey Wheeler)

19   Signature of Alice Neville, Lady Fitzhugh (Fenn's *Original Letters*, vol. 2)

20   Signature of Margaret Neville, Countess of Oxford (Fenn's *Original Letters*, vol. 2)

21   Signature of Katherine Neville, Lady Hastings (Huntington Library, HAP Box 4 (29))

22   Seal of Katherine Neville, Lady Hastings (Huntington Library, HAP Box 4 (29))

Table 1

The Children of Ralph Neville, Earl of Westmoreland and Joan Beaufort

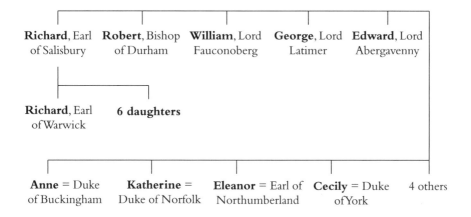

Richard, Earl of Salisbury **Robert**, Bishop of Durham **William**, Lord Fauconoberg **George**, Lord Latimer **Edward**, Lord Abergavenny

Richard, Earl of Warwick **6 daughters**

Anne = Duke of Buckingham **Katherine** = Duke of Norfolk **Eleanor** = Earl of Northumberland **Cecily** = Duke of York 4 others

TABLE 2

THE CHILDREN OF RICHARD NEVILLE, EARL OF SALISBURY

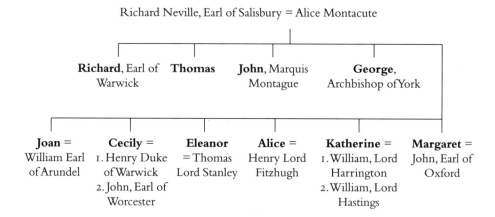

Richard Neville, Earl of Salisbury = Alice Montacute

Richard, Earl of Warwick   **Thomas**   **John**, Marquis Montague   **George**, Archbishop of York

Joan =
William Earl of Arundel

Cecily =
1. Henry Duke of Warwick
2. John, Earl of Worcester

Eleanor = Thomas Lord Stanley

Alice = Henry Lord Fitzhugh

Katherine =
1. William, Lord Harrington
2. William, Lord Hastings

Margaret = John, Earl of Oxford

Table 3

The Kingmaker's Sisters and their Husbands

Joan (d. 1462) m. William Fitzalan, Earl of Arundel (d. 1487)

Cecily (d. 1450) m. 1. Henry Beauchamp, Duke of Warwick (d. 1446)
2. John Tiptoft, Earl of Worcester (ex. 1470)

Eleanor (d. *c.* 1472) m. Thomas, Lord Stanley (d. 1504)

Alice (d. after 1503) m. Henry, Lord Fitzhugh (d. 1472)

Katherine (d. 1503/4) m. 1. William, Lord Harrington (k. 1460)
2. William, Lord Hastings (ex. 1483)

Margaret (d. 1506), m. John de Vere, Earl of Oxford (d. 1513)

TABLE 4

SOME GRANDCHILDREN OF RICHARD NEVILLE, EARL OF SALISBURY

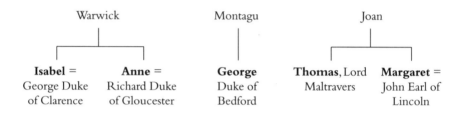

Warwick		Montagu	Joan	
Isabel =	**Anne** =	**George**	**Thomas**, Lord	**Margaret** =
George Duke	Richard Duke	Duke of	Maltravers	John Earl of
of Clarence	of Gloucester	Bedford		Lincoln

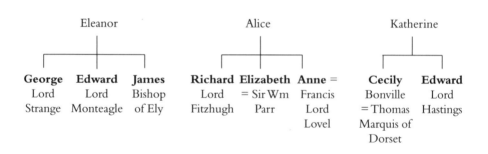

Eleanor			Alice			Katherine	
George	**Edward**	**James**	**Richard**	**Elizabeth**	**Anne** =	**Cecily**	**Edward**
Lord	Lord	Bishop	Lord	= Sir Wm	Francis	Bonville	Lord
Strange	Monteagle	of Ely	Fitzhugh	Parr	Lord	= Thomas	Hastings
					Lovel	Marquis of	
						Dorset	

TABLE 5

THE KINGMAKER, HIS FATHER, HIS BROTHERS-IN-LAW, AND THEIR SONS, IN THE WARS OF THE ROSES

Battle	Yorkist	Lancastrian/Tudor
First St Albans	Salisbury, Warwick	None
Blore Heath	Salisbury	None
Ludford Bridge	Salisbury, Warwick	Arundel, Fitzhugh
Northampton	Warwick	Stanley
Wakefield	Salisbury, Harrington	None
Mortimers Cross	Hastings	
Second St Albans	Warwick, Arundel	Fitzhugh
Towton	Warwick, Arundel, Stanley, Hastings	None
Edgecote	None	Fitzhugh
Losecoat Field	Worcester, Hastings	None
Barnet	Hastings	Warwick, Oxford
Tewkesbury	Hastings	None
Bosworth	Richard Fitzhugh, Thomas Fitzalan	Oxford, Stanley
Stoke	None	Oxford, George Stanley, Edward Hastings

A Note on the Tables

obert Neville, Bishop of Salisbury and Durham (Table 1) is portrayed in some family trees as the second son of the first Earl of Westmoreland and Joan Beaufort, but is said elsewhere to have been their *fifth* son. The confusion arises because three short-lived sons, Thomas, Henry and Cuthbert, were born to the Earl and Countess between the birth of their eldest son Richard, the future Earl of Salisbury, in 1399, and Robert's arrival in 1404. Robert was therefore his parents' fifth son, but only the second to reach maturity. It is incorrect to show William, Lord Fauconberg, George, Lord Latimer, and Edward, Lord Abergavenny (or Bergavenny) as the second, third and fourth sons and Robert as the fifth.

The order of the Kingmaker's sisters is not entirely certain (Table 2). Joan and Cecily were certainly the eldest and second eldest, and Margaret the youngest, but we cannot tell if Eleanor was older than Alice or vice versa. Eleanor, who married Thomas, Lord Stanley, is also said to have been wedded to Edmund Beaufort, Duke of Somerset, who was killed at the first battle of St Albans in 1455 (M. Hicks, *Warwick the Kingmaker* (Oxford, 2002) p. 117; M.J. Bennett, *The Oxford Dictionary of National Biography* (Oxford, 2004) vol. 52, p. 237), but this is a mistake. The Eleanor who married Somerset was a daughter of Richard Beauchamp, Earl of Warwick, not Richard Neville, Earl of Salisbury.

INTRODUCTION

ichard Neville, Earl of Warwick the famous – perhaps infamous – 'Kingmaker' had six sisters: Joan, who was a few years older; Cecily, who was about the same age and who may have been his twin; and Eleanor, Alice, Katherine and Margaret who were younger. They all married wealthy and influential noblemen. Joan's husband was William Fitzalan, Earl of Arundel, while Cecily was espoused first to Henry Beauchamp, Duke of Warwick, and, after his death, to John Tiptoft, Earl of Worcester. Eleanor wed Thomas, Lord Stanley; Alice, Henry, Lord Fitzhugh; Katherine, William, Lord Harrington, and secondly, William, Lord Hastings; and Margaret, John de Vere, Earl of Oxford. These men not infrequently found themselves at odds in the Wars of the Roses, and the ways in which this affected their wives, both as individuals and as part of an extended family, will form a central theme of this book.

It is less easy to weave together the lives of six people than to deal with a single biography, but a major advantage is that we can make more comparisons, and draw more parallels, than would be possible if our focus was limited to just one – or even two – of them. Three of the sisters died comparatively young, Cecily in 1450, Joan in 1462, and Eleanor before 1472, but their remaining siblings survived into the early years of the sixteenth century. Three, Cecily, Alice, and Katherine, were widowed, Cecily and Katherine when they were still young and after only a few years of marriage. They soon remarried, but Alice, who was older when Lord Fitzhugh died, remained single for more than thirty years, and Katherine outlived Lord Hastings, her second husband, by over twenty. They all bore at least one of their husbands a child, although Anne, Cecily's daughter, and George, Margaret's son, predeceased them. Joan, Eleanor, and Katherine each had a number of children, and Alice as many as eleven.

The sisters' husbands, a duke, three earls, and four barons, would have worked harmoniously with the King and with one another in normal circumstances, but these were not 'normal' times. Henry, Duke of Warwick, Cecily's first husband, died in 1446 before the outbreak of the 'Wars of the Roses', but of the others, three, the Earl of Worcester and Katherine's husbands Lords Harrington and Hastings, were dedicated Yorkists who all met violent deaths. Margaret's husband, the Earl of Oxford, was a staunch Lancastrian; Henry, Lord Fitzhugh, seems to have been committed primarily to Warwick, his brother-in-law; the Earl of Arundel fought for the Yorkists at second St Albans and Towton but thereafter played little part in either war or politics; and Thomas, Lord Stanley managed to accommodate himself to whichever party governed by making himself indispensable to all. Some who became widowers, the Earl of Worcester and Lord Stanley for example, soon married other noblewomen, but the Earl of Arundel did not take another wife although he outlived Joan Neville by a quarter of a century. The sisters' own social network helped to bind the family together, and may have prevented their husbands' relationships from collapsing altogether during periods of stress.

There is no modern – or even older – biography of any of the sisters in any of the standard collections, and a trawl through the back numbers of the *Ricardian* (the journal of the Richard III Society) produced not a single article devoted to them. They feature to a greater or, more usually, lesser, extent in biographies of Warwick, their brother,[1] and are noticed in the short 'lives' of their husbands included in *The Oxford Dictionary of National Biography* and *The Complete Peerage*.[2] Eleanor is briefly mentioned in Barry Coward's *The Stanleys, Lords Stanley and Earls of Derby* (Manchester, 1983), and Cecily finds a place in R.J. Mitchell's biography of her second husband *John Tiptoft* (London, 1938), but they have never been studied in depth. We must therefore begin almost from scratch, and some interesting material is available when we *scratch* beneath the surface. Only a little personal information survives for the Countess of Arundel, and the Duchess of Warwick and Countess of Worcester; but there are two manuscript letters written by Lady Stanley, two sent by Lady Fitzhugh that have been printed, and a number of documents that illuminate the lives of Lady Hastings and the Countess of Oxford. Only Katherine Hastings has left an extant will – it is doubtful if some of the sisters, particularly those who died in their husband's lifetimes, ever made them – but we do possess the last testament of her husband William, executed by Richard, Duke of Gloucester in 1483, together with those of the Earl of Oxford, who outlived his wife Margaret by some seven years, and Thomas, Lord Stanley who survived Eleanor by more than thirty. Accounts seldom exist from so remote a period, but the Huntington Library holds a fragment of one of Katherine's arrears rolls, and there are some references to Margaret in a receiver-general's account and in a household book kept by her husband. It is sometimes argued that it is unrealistic to attempt biographies of those who lived in the Middle Ages because the detailed, personal information that would make this possible is simply not available; but these and other papers allow us to glimpse the sisters' personalities and relationships, and tell us something about the dramatic changes of fortune that could beset ladies at the highest levels of society in the later fifteenth century. Their husbands and sons may have reaped the rewards – and sometimes lost their heads – in the process, but it was invariably wives and mothers who smoothed troubled waters while they awaited better days.

I would like to thank the following who provided information in response to my inquiries: Anne Marie Anderton (The John Rylands University Library, University of Manchester), Bruce Jackson (County Archivist, Lancashire Record Office), Mary L. Robertson (Chief Curator of Manuscripts, Huntington Library), Sara Rodger (Assistant Librarian, Arundel Castle), D.J. Salmon (Assistant Archivist, North Yorkshire County Record Office), John Ashdown-Hill, Lesley Boatwright, Kenneth Hillier, James Ross, J.R. Wignall, and not least students who attended courses based on the book at Vaughan College, Leicester, and the Doddridge Centre,

Northampton, and who shared their thoughts on the sisters with me. I am particularly grateful to Professor Tony Pollard for reading my typescript and suggesting a number of improvements, to Geoffrey Wheeler for providing some of the illustrations and for his constant interest in the project, and to my wife, Joyce, who, although not a historian, helped in many other ways.

David Baldwin

1

THE NEVILLE FAMILY

he Nevilles are an example – perhaps the example *par excellence* – of how a minor aristocratic medieval family could rise from relative obscurity to enjoy a place at the heart of both the royal house and government. A dynasty that could produce a male heir in each generation could hardly fail to add to its acres and influence as rivals and relatives alike were extinguished; but this needed to be complemented by judicious marriages to heiresses and by an ability to sniff which way the political wind was blowing. Rich rewards were available to those who successfully negotiated the pitfalls, but disaster awaited any who were found wanting. Some heiresses were the survivors of what McFarlane has called 'enfeebled stocks'[1] (the result of their families intermarrying too often), and a bad political decision, be it to support the reigning king or a rival claimant, could result in execution and forfeiture. An attainted heir might slowly work his way back into royal favour, but his prospects would have been seriously damaged in the short term.

Many noble families were able to accomplish some of these things for part of the time, but few could rival the almost flawless progress of the Nevilles. In generation after generation they wedded heiresses, sired large numbers of children by them, and accumulated a rich landed estate centred on the castles of Raby and Brancepeth in County Durham and Middleham and Sheriff Hutton in Yorkshire. It was in 1397, in the aftermath of his coup against those noblemen who had resisted his will ten years earlier, that Richard II raised Ralph Neville, the then head of the family, to the earldom of Westmoreland,[2] but Ralph did not allow his gratitude to cloud his view of the political situation or take his eye off the main chance. When Henry Bolingbroke landed at Ravenspur in July 1399, Ralph, the husband of Henry's half-sister Joan Beaufort, was among the first to join him, and he bore the royal sceptre when the usurper was crowned king as Henry IV. He proved his loyalty by resisting the rebellions of the Percies in 1403 and the Duke of Norfolk and Archbishop Scrope two years later, a sequence of events that effectively eliminated his main rivals and further enhanced his authority in the restless north.

Earl Ralph married twice and fathered some twenty-three children, nine by his first wife Margaret Stafford and fourteen more by the Countess Joan. John, his eldest son by his first wife, had first claim on his father's title, but these older children of the first brood lacked the royal connections of their younger siblings of the half-blood. It was presumably thanks to Joan's influence that Richard, her eldest son, married Alice Montacute, heiress to the earldom of Salisbury, and his brother Robert, the churchman of the family, became first Bishop of Salisbury and then Bishop of Durham. Four other sons secured heiresses to baronies, becoming Lords Fauconberg, St Maur, Latimer, and Bergavenny, while four daughters were contracted to the Dukes of Buckingham, Norfolk and York, and the Earl of Northumberland. These arrangements would, in due course, help Norfolk and Northumberland to recover the titles forfeited by their brother and grandfather in Henry IV's reign, and there were doubtless others who found that a connection with Earl Ralph and his countess could improve their relations with the Crown or enhance their prospects. It was the culmination of many years of patient planning and hard work.

When Earl Ralph died in 1425 he left his Durham estates to his grandson Ralph (John, his eldest son, had predeceased him), but the Yorkshire lands were settled on the Countess Joan. She had no intention of allowing them to pass to the offspring of her husband's first wife, and the scene was set for decades of friction between the 'senior' and 'junior' branches of the family.

John had rather surprisingly acquiesced in this arrangement, and Ralph the younger, who was still a minor, could do nothing to prevent it; but the latter did not conceal his displeasure after he came of age in 1429. In 1435 the Chancellor was informed that 'owing to the grievous differences which have arisen between Ralph Earl of Westmoreland and his brothers John and Thomas on the one hand, and Joan Dowager-Countess of Westmoreland and her son Richard Earl of Salisbury on the other hand, [who] have of late assembled, by manner of war and insurrection, great routs and companies upon the field, which have done all manner of great offences as well in slaughter and destruction of the King's lieges as otherwise, which things are greatly against the estate and weal and peace of this realm'[3]. The Privy Council appointed three arbitrators and the differences were patched up for the moment: but the problem is typical of the disputes that could beset an inheritance when a man reared two families. The eldest son could not have everything, and his half-brothers could never have enough!

The second Earl Ralph continued to contest the arrangement after his step-grandmother died in 1440, but could make little headway against Salisbury whose royal connections and superior service both in France and on the Scottish border always stood him in good stead with the Crown. Another 'compromise' in 1443 all but settled the matter in Salisbury's favour, and Westmoreland would have been poorer than some fourteenth-century lords of Raby if he had not inherited lands from his mother, Elizabeth Holland. Salisbury's power had previously been drawn from his wife's Montacute estates in the West Country, but his new possessions, the valuable lordships of Middleham, Sheriff Hutton, and Penrith in Westmoreland (which the King had given his parents when they married), made him a force to be reckoned with in northern England. It would be the younger Nevilles who would henceforward dispute the dominance of the region with the Percies, while the elder 'senior' branch of the family played only a supporting role.

II

Richard Neville, Earl of Salisbury proved himself a worthy successor to his father, not only in war and politics but also in his ability to raise a large family. Joan, his eldest daughter, the future Countess of Arundel, was born before 2 November 1424, followed by Cecily who would one day become Duchess of Warwick. Richard, the future 'Kingmaker', made his entry into the world in 1428, and was soon joined by three younger brothers, Thomas, John, sometime Earl of Northumberland and Marquess Montagu, and George, who became Bishop of Exeter and Archbishop of York. Two short-lived sons, Ralph and Robert, and three more daughters, Eleanor, who would marry Thomas, Lord Stanley, Alice, who would espouse Henry, Lord Fitzhugh, and Katherine, whose two husbands, William Bonville, Lord Harrington, and William, Lord Hastings, would both die violently, were born between 1433 and 1442, while Margaret, who was destined to become Countess of Oxford, completed the brood in about 1443. Twelve children in nineteen years sounds a very large number, but was by no means unusual at this period. Richard, Duke of York, and his duchess Cecily, Salisbury's sister and brother-in-law, also produced twelve children between 1439 and 1455 (although only eight of these reached maturity), and York's son, Edward IV, sired ten in fourteen years. Peasant women knew that prolonged breastfeeding would delay another pregnancy, but great ladies who employed wet-nurses did not have this option. The Church tried to discourage sex by banning it on Sundays, throughout Lent, and for almost half the year in total, but there is no evidence that fewer children were conceived.

The birth of each child would have been preceded and followed by a sequence of well-established customs, beginning when the mother-to-be 'took her chamber' – a well-furnished room with subdued lighting – about a month before she was due. She entered an exclusively female world from which even the male doctors who usually attended her were excluded, and depended on the skills of midwives aided by sacred relics borrowed for the occasion. A successful delivery would be an occasion for great relief and rejoicing, but the mother would not be permitted to join in the celebrations until she had been ritually purified by the ceremony of 'churching' forty days (six weeks) later. The Countess Alice and her children would have enjoyed the best care then available, but the process was inevitably hazardous and there may have been unrecorded stillbirths or deaths within a few hours.

The sisters' first rite of passage, indeed almost the first act of their lives, was baptism, since babies who died unbaptised risked being caught in a kind of limbo between heaven and hell and their souls 'lost'.[4] Lay persons were allowed to anoint a child's head with water and christen him or her in the name of the Trinity if death seemed imminent, but only a priest could decide if the makeshift ceremony had been performed adequately and the infant received into the Church and 'saved'. All Salisbury's children would have been carried to the font literally within hours of making their entry into the world.[5] Godparents – two fathers and one mother for a boy, the reverse for a girl – would have been chosen well in advance, almost certainly with a view to creating a formal relationship between the infant and persons of some consequence. Today it is invariably grandparents who supplement the role of the parents in a child's upbringing and godparents (where they exist) do little or nothing; but in the medieval era it was the godparents who were charged with protecting and instructing the infant, particularly if the parents became incapacitated. The gifts the godparents gave their new charges at their baptisms would have been generous, in keeping with their rank in society, and the parents doubtless hoped they would be followed by more favours as the years passed.

We do not know the identities of Salisbury's daughters' godparents, but the custom by which the most senior gave, or was invited to give, her name to the infant may afford some clues.[6] Joan, the eldest, was almost certainly named for her grandmother, Joan Beaufort, and Cecily, Eleanor and Katherine for their aunts, Salisbury's sisters, the Duchess of York, the Countess of Northumberland, and the Duchess of Norfolk. Margaret's godmother may have been Margaret Beauchamp, eldest daughter of Richard Beauchamp, Earl of Warwick, and wife of John Talbot, Earl of Shrewsbury. Salisbury had entered into a close relationship with Earl Richard in 1436 (see below), and the families did not fall out over the inheritance until after 1449. Curiously, no child was called Anne after Salisbury's other prominent sister, Anne, Duchess of Buckingham, and there does not appear to have been an Alice among the family's close relatives. Possibly Alice was named for her mother, Alice Montacute, although it was Duchess Anne who lifted her from the font.

III

Salisbury's offspring would have begun their lives as part of a growing and peripatetic nursery that moved slowly around his Countess's principal manors in Wessex. They doubtless visited their grandmother, Joan, at Middleham and Sheriff Hutton, and began to live there more permanently after their father inherited the estates in 1440. Their earliest years would have been spent in the care of servants, partly because their parents were frequently absent on their own and the King's business, and because convention dictated that noble ladies did not nurture their children on a day-to-day basis. Nurses and tutors became, in effect, surrogate mothers and fathers, but there was a sense of belonging based on the notion that the family's collective prosperity required the full cooperation of all its members. Boys and girls were expected to accede to their parents' wishes – and could expect harsh punishment if they objected – because the Church taught that to resist or disobey them was sinful. There are no specific examples of how the Nevilles disciplined their offspring, but the law did not protect children from parents who abused them and the principle of 'spare the rod and spoil the child' was applied throughout noble and gentle society. They may not have suffered like Elizabeth Paston who was 'betyn onys [once] in the weke or twyes, and som tyme tywes on o [one] day, and hir hed broken in to or thre places'[7] when she refused to marry the man her parents had chosen for her, but they knew the rules and the consequences of breaking them. Those in charge of noble households tried to maintain a quiet, ordered, atmosphere, particularly during mealtimes, but children were probably no less boisterous than they are today.

Formal lessons – in Latin and French, with a smattering of law and mathematics – began at the age of four, and became part of their regimen for the next few years. A typical day began with mass in the family chapel followed by a light breakfast of bread, cheese and ale (at six or seven o'clock according to the season) and then serious study until dinner at perhaps ten or eleven. Later, there would be more enjoyable lessons, riding, archery, dancing, learning to play a musical instrument or perhaps sewing and embroidery in the company of the ladies of the household. Supper followed in the late afternoon after Evensong, and then there would be time to play games such as 'buck hide', a form of hide-and-seek, or to amuse themselves with dolls before bedtime. It was a communal life in which privacy was almost non-existent. The girls would have slept together, the younger with the elder, and innocence would have been lost at an early age.

The most traumatic moment of their childhoods came when, at some time between the ages of seven and ten, they were sent into other noble households, the boys to learn the profession of arms and the girls the practical skills of a great lady. A system that separated children from their families this early may appear harsh by modern standards, but was probably no harsher than sending a child of similar age to a modern boarding school. Surviving letters show that homesickness was a common problem, but they undoubtedly learned self-reliance and formed friendships that would stand them in good stead later. The boys received a more comprehensive education (rather unfairly perhaps, since both sexes were expected to become competent estate managers), but all were 'grown-up' and ready to enter the adult world by the time they reached their early teens. Where Salisbury's children went, when, and for how long, is entirely unknown to us, but none of the girls entered a convent. Noble fathers often gave a younger daughter to religion – two of the elder Ralph Neville's daughters had entered the Minories in London, and Edward IV arranged for his youngest child, Bridget, to become a nun at Dartford – but the sisters were all destined for secular life.

It follows from this that Salisbury and his wife did not form a close bond with their children in infancy – that would come later – but the children would probably have seen little more of them had they remained at home. The Earl served as warden of both the western and eastern marches towards Scotland until 1435, and was also employed as captain of Berwick and as an ambassador to the King of Scots. He campaigned in Normandy with the Duke of York in the summer of 1436, and was appointed to the royal

Council on his return to England. Sir Charles Oman remarks that his attendance at Council meetings was regular and 'exemplary', but observes that his new role would have kept him in London (and away from his family in northern England) 'for the greater part of the next ten years'.[8] His countess was by his side for much of this period and would only have seen her children at family gatherings, or possibly if one of them suffered a serious, life-threatening illness. The youngsters were probably in awe of their parents on the rare occasions they met them, and felt respect and admiration rather than love.

IV

It is likely that Salisbury began to think in terms of finding suitable marriage partners for his children from almost the moment they were born. In 1436 it was agreed that Cecily, his second daughter, would marry Henry, Lord Despenser, son and heir of the Earl of Warwick, and that his eldest son Richard would simultaneously wed Warwick's daughter, Anne. The arrangement would have worked mainly to Cecily's advantage if all the parties had enjoyed their normal life spans; but Henry and his only daughter were both dead by 1449, and the real beneficiary was Richard Neville the younger who became Earl of Warwick in right of his wife. Joan, Salisbury's eldest daughter, married William Fitzalan, Earl of Arundel after 17 August 1438, but there was then an interlude of some fifteen years before Thomas, his second son, wed Maud Stanhope, Lady Willoughby in 1453.

Salisbury had undoubtedly done his best for his older children, but the negotiations had not always been easy or inexpensive. He had to promise to pay the Earl of Warwick the large sum of 4,700 marks (£3,233.66) before Warwick would allow his heir Henry to marry Cecily (Salisbury was clearly the suppliant in the matter), and the marriage of the young Earl of Arundel had to be bought from the Crown. Neither Richard, who was seven, nor Cecily, a year or two his senior, can have had any say in their parents' arrangements and would not have been asked if they liked their intended partners or wanted to spend the rest of their lives with them. It had long been accepted that a marriage was valid only if the contacting parties consented to it, but was it possible, or practical, to ask infants if they agreed to something they would not have understood until they were older? The Church overcame this by allowing that children could be married at seven on condition that girls could repudiate the agreement at twelve and boys at fourteen, the ages at which they were deemed to reach puberty. A marriage that had been arranged years earlier could be annulled if the young couple refused to consummate it when they were able, but again, only the bravest of sons or daughters would have dared reject plans designed to benefit the whole family. A few fearless souls may have stood up to their parents, but the majority undoubtedly acquiesced.

So far, so good, but another potential difficulty was that so many Nevilles had married into the ranks of the higher nobility in previous generations that some unions that were politically and financially desirable fell within the prohibited degrees. These were widely drawn in the Middle Ages – fourth cousins and nearer relatives could not legally marry – and a papal dispensation would be needed to overcome them and ensure that any children born to the couple were legitimate. Such concerns would not have troubled the average peasant, but a lord whose heirs might be challenged by ambitious rivals could not be too careful. Salisbury probably felt a sense of relief as each child was suitably and lawfully wedded, but their happiness – whether they loved, or would grow to love, their life's partners – would scarcely have entered his mind.

A twelve-year-old girl who could consent to marriage had clearly reached the age of discretion in the Church's eyes, but other responsibilities were assumed at different ages. She would not be permitted to swear an oath or give evidence in court until she was between fourteen and sixteen, and was unlikely to be punished by the criminal law until she was thought old enough to know what she was doing.[9] Sometimes, a child who had 'accidentally' killed another youngster would be imprisoned until the case could be heard by a travelling justice; but the 'offender' was normally pardoned unless it was clear that he or she had intended to cause serious injury. It is unlikely that any of the sisters ever found themselves in this situation, but serious accidents were inevitable in a society of open wells, boiling pots and unguarded fires.

V

The double wedding of 1436 amply repaid the time and money that Salisbury had invested in the marriages, but only because careful planning and good fortune walked hand in hand. If Henry, Cecily's husband, had died without succeeding to his father's Beauchamp lands then the co-heiresses would have been the Earl's three daughters by his first wife and the only daughter of his second marriage, young Richard's spouse Anne. The Countess Isabel, Anne's mother, had also been married twice, and the heirs to her Despenser estates would in these circumstances have been Anne and her daughter by her first husband. But Henry *had* inherited – he survived his father by seven years before dying in 1446 – and this allowed Anne, his only sister of the full blood, to claim the whole inheritance after Henry's infant daughter died in 1449. Young Richard became Earl of Warwick in right of his wife, objections to their windfall being effectively stymied by the fact that the husbands of the two eldest half-sisters, John Talbot, Earl of Shrewsbury and Edmund Beaufort, Duke of Somerset were busy defending Normandy, and the third, George Neville, Lord Latimer, was a lunatic whose estates were in the custody of his brother, the Earl of Salisbury. The three ladies had to settle for a total of nine manors while a moiety of the Despenser lands was preserved for George, the son of Anne's now deceased half-sister on her mother's side of the family. Custody of this was granted to Cecily and her second husband the Earl of Worcester, but Worcester surrendered it to Warwick two months before his wife died in July 1450.[10] George's rights were ignored when he came of age in 1457, and Anne was cynically declared to be the sole heir of her mother in Edward IV's first parliament in 1461.

Henry would have had a major role in the Wars of the Roses if he had lived for at least another decade, but alone among the sisters' husbands he was destined to play no part at all. He was still only twenty-one when he died at Hanley Castle in Worcestershire (where he had also been born), on 11 June 1446, but had already been of service to the Lancastrian government. He was a royal councillor by 1441 (when he would have been only sixteen), and clearly stood high in royal favour when Henry VI raised him to the dukedom of Warwick in April 1445. The *Rous Roll* says that Pope Nicholas V invited him to become 'captain of his wars' (a mistake, since Nicholas did not succeed until 1447), and some of Rous's other compliments are, as Christine Carpenter notes, 'somewhat out of keeping with what is known of his career'. Did he really go to confession every day as Rous alleges, and did he 'suffer no officer of his to oppress any man', dismissing them if they refused to amend?[11] It is more probable that his piety was conventional and his love of justice always subject to the needs of his coffers and lands.

VI

There can be little doubt that by the end of the fifth decade of the fifteenth century the younger branch of the Neville family had become a powerful voice in English politics. Thomas, Lord St Maur had died prematurely, but during the 1450s five brothers, Richard, Earl of Salisbury, Robert, Bishop of Durham, William, Lord Fauconberg, the mentally unstable George, Lord Latimer and Edward, Lord Bergavenny were members of the house of peers together with their brothers-in-law of Norfolk, Buckingham, York and Northumberland. Salisbury's own star may have waned; but this was more than compensated by the rapid rise of his son Warwick, and the family could look forward to a bright future in the next generation. None of them could have guessed that the conflicts of the Wars of the Roses would lead to the deaths of Salisbury, Warwick, Salisbury's younger sons Thomas and John, three of his brothers-in-law, and three of his daughters' (and Warwick's sisters') husbands. Civil war is always brutal, and the Nevilles, more prominent and politically active than many, would pay a proportionately higher price.

2

THE SISTERS' ENGLAND

What was it like, the England into which the sisters were born, grew up and, in due course, married? Very little of what we know comes from the pens of English writers because they seldom troubled to record what, for them, was everyday and commonplace; but we are fortunate to have two accounts composed by Italian visitors at the beginning of the sixteenth century when three of the sisters were still living. One, Polydore Vergil of Urbino, was a noted author who wrote a history of England for Henry VII; the other, a noble Venetian whose name is lost to us, spent some of his leisure time writing what he called *A Relation of the Island of England … about the year 1500.* There is also Erasmus, Thomas More's friend, who told a correspondent that 'did you but know the blessings of Britain you would clap wings to your feet and run thither'.[1] However, his enthusiasm was dampened when, on leaving the country, he was relieved of all his money in accordance with an old law forbidding the export of bullion that King Henry had recently reactivated! Their accounts tell us how they saw the English, but not, of course, how the English saw themselves.

Vergil notes that Britain is made up of four 'partes', or regions 'whereof the one is inhabited of Englishmen, the other of Scottes, the third of

Walleshemen, the fowerthe of Cornishe people', and that England is sub-divided into thirty-nine counties, ten between the Thames and the sea, sixteen between the Thames and the Trent, six 'towardes Walles and the west partes', and seven nearer Scotland. It is a generally prosperous land, 'most frutefull on this side of the river of Humber, for on the other side it somewhat to muche abowndethe in mountaynes', a view echoed by the Venetian who describes England as 'all diversified by pleasant undulating hills, and beautiful valleys, nothing being to be seen but agreeable woods, or extensive meadows, or lands in cultivation; and the greatest plenty of water springing everywhere'.[2] There was mineral wealth – contemporaries mention quarries of stone, slate and alabaster together with coal and lead mines – and the Venetian remarks on the 'immense profusion of every comestible animal' ... riches exceeded only by 'an enormous number of sheep which yield quantities of wool of the best quality'.[3] The forests, still extensive in places, are, he says, diminishing, and the fertile soil produces a sufficiency of wheat, oats, barley and pulses. Nothing is imported from abroad except wine.

The principal arteries of the kingdom were still the roads built by the Romans centuries earlier and the numerous rivers. They gave access to the towns and villages that lay along them, settlements surrounded by their own arable land and pasture, still mainly unenclosed, open, fields. Here and there were dotted the great houses of lords and gentlemen, but many of the old castles were decaying. 'In the more settled parts of the kingdom a few royal castles still retained some remnant of their departed glory',[4] but others, together with many city walls and defences, now lacked maintenance. Most towns and cities had, in any case, expanded beyond their original fortifications, and their occupants lived largely without fear.

The Italian visitors thought the countryside sparsely populated and the towns much smaller than in their native country. It has been estimated that by Henry VIII's reign Norwich had a population not exceeding 12,000, Bristol 10,000, Exeter, York and Salisbury 8,000 each, and Coventry 7,500. Smaller places such as King's Lynn, Oxford, Cambridge, Ipswich, Canterbury, Colchester and Great Yarmouth fluctuated between 2,600 and 5,000, but the number of inhabitants of other places was significantly less.[5] They were all dwarfed by London, which may have had as many as 60,000 residents, and which impressed natives and foreigners alike. London Bridge, regarded by many as a wonder of the world, was longer than its modern successor and stood on twenty piles of squared stones joined with arches. So many houses had been built on it that it looked more like a street than a bridge proper, and it facilitated the commerce of the city almost as much as the Thames that ran beneath it. Successful businessmen, merchants and city companies, had built fine halls on sites still associated with them, and the Venetian was particularly impressed that 'in one single street, named the Strand [actually Cheapside, or Goldsmith's Row], there are fifty-two goldsmith's shops, so rich and full of silver vessels, great and small, that in all the shops in Milan, Rome, Venice, and Florence put together, I do not think there would be found so many of the magnificence that are to be seen in London.'[6] There was squalor too, of course, but the city was clearly a bustling, thriving metropolis in the sisters' day.

Houses were built of whatever material happened to be plentiful in the locality – stone in Sleaford, wood in Leicester and brick in Hull where clay was obtainable – but one building that was invariably constructed of stone was the local church. Every settlement worthy of the name had one, and quite modest towns had several – Northampton had seven within the town proper for example, while nearby Leicester boasted six.[7] London, dominated by St Paul's set on its hill, had no fewer than ninety-seven parish churches and a score of great religious houses – Professor Mackie remarks that 'the traveller approaching the city must have beheld a very forest of spires and on entering must have been greeted with a cheerful clamour of bells'.[8] It has been estimated that two-thirds of parish churches were built or re-built during the fifteenth century – the East Anglian 'wool' churches are the prime example – and not only rebuilt but endowed with innumerable donations of furniture, rich vestments, plate and jewels. Those unable to construct entire churches might found chantries within them, while others gave money to finance hospitals and schools.

It might be supposed that this great re-building programme was at least partly necessitated by the depredations of the Wars of the Roses, but there is little evidence of serious damage. Professor Goodman has estimated that forces were in arms for only 428 days (the equivalent of sixty-one weeks) between 1455 and 1485, and although nine major battles were fought within this period there were scarcely any sieges or urban conflicts.[9] Those who lived near a battlefield or close to a route taken by an army may have experienced some temporary disruption, but there was none of the devastation that had blighted earlier civil wars. The 'anarchy' of Stephen's reign had wrought havoc upon Lincoln (for example), and Leicester was so thoroughly sacked when its earl, Robert Blanchemains, rebelled against Henry II that former residential areas in one parish became orchards, and once busy streets were thereafter green lanes. Coventry was briefly besieged when the Kingmaker refused to leave the safety of its walls in 1471, but Edward IV was not prepared to waste time assaulting the place, still less starve it into surrender. Similarly, the 'old' nobility, was not, as K.B. McFarlane pointed out, destroyed by the Wars since the majority of those who fell or were executed left heirs to succeed them; but there was a short-term problem in the sense that many of these heirs were minors and it would be years – many years in some cases – before they could participate in war and politics.[10] Overall, the situation was not as bad as it might have been, but it would still affect the lives of five of Warwick's sisters to a greater or lesser extent.

The Black Death of the previous century had laid its deadly hand on both urban and rural communities, and the population remained depressed for much of the sisters' lifetimes. It had plummeted from about 5 million before 1348–49 to 2.5 million by 1377, and declined further to perhaps only 2 million in 1450. Disease may have been the prime factor, but there is also evidence that ordinary people were choosing to marry later than they had a century earlier and were accordingly having fewer children. Many couples now delayed marriage until their mid-twenties (the mid- or late teens had been the norm previously), and it has been estimated that 24.2 per cent of all males died unmarried during the period 1430–80 while 49 per cent of those who did marry left no male heir. This situation prevailed until nearer the end of the century, when, it seems, a larger number of marriages contributed to a rising birth rate and the population slowly began to recover. But it still stood at only 2.26 million in 1525.[11]

The realm was governed by a king who was his own general and foreign minister, but who could not make law nor tax his subjects without their consent in Parliament. He was helped in this process by some fifty to sixty lay peers, dukes, earls and barons, together with the occasional marquis and viscount, and, at a lower level, by 350–400 knights and perhaps 5,000 squires and gentlemen. They collectively made up what we may term the secular 'aristocracy', and their wealth and authority was matched only by that of the religious hierarchy. The Venetian speaks of 'enormously rich Benedictine, Carthusian, and Cistertian monasteries ... more like baronial palaces than religious houses',[12] and bishops and senior clergy still filled important posts in both Church and state. Magna Carta had confirmed the Church's jurisdictional independence and right to self-regulation, but most English clergy found it possible to serve two masters even when, on occasion, there was conflict between royal and papal interests. Church and state had combined to suppress the Lollard heresy in the generation before the sisters entered the world, and their shared interests far outweighed any temporary difficulties that might arise.

The later medieval Church was clearly in need of reform and its critics were becoming increasingly vocal, but it was sustained by the fact that a worldly priest remained a man of God who might still hold the key to salvation. Chaucer's clerical pilgrims may be figures of fun but they were clearly recognisable; and even the best of them, the 'poure persone [parson] of a toun', might leave much to be desired in reality. Canon law required parish clergy to say the daily liturgies, visit those who were ill, preach at least four times a year and hear the confessions of parishioners at least once. They were further charged to lead upright lives, set an example to their people, and ensure that their relations with women were beyond reproach. Some may indeed have adhered to these high precepts, but there were many who made mistresses of their housekeepers and found it more profitable to cultivate their glebeland than to preach or visit the sick. Peasants who paid tithes felt that they were not getting value for money, but endowments were not always adequate and some vicars and rectors probably had no alternative but to hold more than one 'living' or raise money by other methods. Many had little time for what we might term the more 'social' aspects of their ministry, and parishioners who were unable to work or who found themselves in other difficulties would have looked mainly to their manorial overlord, or perhaps to a nearby abbey, for assistance. People of standing could join a gild or confraternity, the equivalent of a modern friendly society, in which the members 'looked after' one another; but the underlying philosophy was that everyone had a duty to look after him- or herself.

The Venetian was clearly impressed by the English 'establishment', and devoted a good deal of space to the upper classes and to those who were climbing the ladder of society in his writings. They are, he says:

> for the most part, both men and women of all ages, handsome and well proportioned ... great lovers of themselves, and of everything belonging to them. They think that there are no other men than themselves and no other world but England; and whenever they see a handsome foreigner, they say that 'he looks like an Englishman', and that "it is a great pity that he should not be an Englishman"; and when they partake of any delicacy with a foreigner, they ask him, 'whether such a thing is made in *their* country?' They take great pleasure in having a quantity of excellent victuals, and also in remaining a long time at table, being very sparing of wine when they drink it at their own expense [!]. Few people keep wine in their own houses, but buy it, for the most part, at a tavern; and when they mean to drink a great deal, they go to the tavern, and this is done not only by the men, but by ladies of distinction. They think that no greater honour can be conferred, or received, than to invite others to eat with them, or to be invited themselves; and they would sooner give five or six ducats to provide an entertainment for a person, than a groat to assist him in any distress.
>
> They all wear very fine clothes, are extremely polite in their language, [and] have the incredible courtesy of remaining with their heads uncovered, with an admirable grace, whilst they talk to each other. They are gifted with good understandings, and are very quick at every thing they apply their minds to, [although] few, excepting the clergy, are addicted to the study of letters. They all attend mass every day, the women carrying long rosaries in their hands and any who can read taking the office of our Lady with them.

They give liberal alms and are good Christians in other respects, although some still incline to unorthodoxy or are not slow to voice their criticisms. There are, he says, 'many who have various opinions concerning religion', or behave oddly to his way of thinking:

They have a very high reputation in arms ... but I have it on the best information that when the war is raging most furiously, they will seek for good eating, and all their other comforts, without thinking of what harm might befall them. They have an antipathy to foreigners, and imagine that they never come into their island but to make themselves masters of it, and to usurp their goods; neither have they any sincere and solid friendships among themselves, insomuch that they do not trust each other to discuss either public or private affairs together. And although their dispositions are somewhat licentious, I have never noticed any one, either at court or amongst the lower orders, to be in love; whence one must necessarily conclude, either that the English are the most discreet lovers in the world, or that they are incapable of love. I say this of the men, for I understand it is quite the contrary with the women, who are very violent in their passions. Howbeit the English keep a very jealous guard over their wives, though any thing may be compensated in the end, by the power of money.

He also notices the legal system and remarks that 'there is no country in the world where there are so many thieves and robbers as in England; insomuch, that few venture to go alone in the country, excepting in the middle of the day, and fewer still in the towns at night, and least of all in London'.[13] How little some things change!

II

Our late medieval forbears were clearly not unlike ourselves in some matters and, like us, were living through an era in which the old was constantly giving way to the new. In 1300 the 'peerage' had consisted of those men – usually, though not exclusively, royal tenants-in-chief, and usually numbering fewer than 100 out of a total of some 2,000 eligible tenants-in-chief – who were summoned to attend Parliament, the summons being issued – or withheld – entirely at the King's discretion according to how highly the recipient stood in his estimation at that particular moment. Many men were summoned but once or twice, and sometimes not even to consecutive parliaments;

others were called regularly but were not succeeded by their sons. However, after 1350, without any constitutional or legal landmarks, and without any notable precedents to serve as guideposts, the peerage came to consist of a regular group, all of whom were nearly always summoned. There were fewer of them – only forty-six in 1400 as opposed to ninety-nine in 1313 – but in a growing number of cases it was becoming accepted that the person who inherited the lands of someone who had formerly sat in Parliament inherited the right to a parliamentary writ of summons as well. Successive kings must have felt that the advantages of continuity and heredity outweighed the dangers posed by permanently entrenching the barons in the machinery of government; but henceforth, they would exercise only limited authority over which individuals became peers of the realm.

It may be for this reason that from 1387 onwards suitable candidates were enobled by royal charter or letters patent, as well as by parliamentary writ of summons. Heads of families who had simply survived (and inherited the lands of less fortunate relatives who had died) together with those who had married wealthy heiresses inevitably caught the royal eye, as did those who rendered conspicuously good service. We might suppose that survival (rearing a least one son in each generation) was quite straightforward; but a quarter of noble families, on average, died out in the male line every twenty-five years. Some succumbed to illnesses for which there were no remedies while others fell victim to war or politics; but the underlying problem was probably too much inter-marriage within a comparatively small group of leading families. Noblemen who could not father sons on their wives often had no difficulty begetting them by their mistresses, and it is likely that genetic factors were at least partly to blame.

McFarlane has calculated that in 1300 there were 136 families whose head had by then received at least one personal writ of summons to Parliament from Edward I and whose descendants can by traced, to which must be added 221 families whose heads received a similar writ during the course of the next two centuries. He estimates that only 61 out of a total of 357, most of them families established fairly recently, survived in unbroken male descent until 1500, and a mere 16 of them were descended from the original 136.[14] The situation was not quite as bleak as these figures suggest because from about 1400 the husband of a sole noble heiress was invariably granted the title that had belonged to her late father, and the growth of entail (the practice by which the bulk of the estates were settled on a particular male relative to allow him to claim the title, often to the detriment of daughters and their husbands) likewise prevented others from falling into abeyance. Kings also helped to replenish the ranks of the nobility by creating new peers, even though this sometimes obliged them to provide lesser men with enough lands to maintain their enhanced status, and added to the risk that certain lords would become what was usually described as 'over-mighty'. Five kings were overthrown by baronial opposition between 1399 and 1485, and yet Henry VI created fifteen new earls after 1447 and Edward IV made thirteen between 1461 and 1469. If the members of the higher nobility were such obstacles to good government, such natural enemies of the royal authority, why didn't sensible kings simply let them die out? The answer is that some noblemen were members of the royal family – the failure of the royal line was always regarded as a greater danger than any threat posed by ambitious heirs – and that although there *were* noble-inspired rebellions it is equally true that for much of this period the kings had no better, more hard-working servants, both in peace and war. A monarchy with no standing army, no police force, the most rudimentary of bureaucracies and only limited financial resources, could not govern without the local influence and authority of the aristocracy: and they themselves *wanted* to serve, because service was the only means by which they could ensure continuous access to the royal patronage upon which they and their dependants relied. Even lords who had rebelled and forfeited their lands could work their way back into royal favour if the king thought it was better to harness their local influence than to appoint someone new to the region – someone who would need time to 'play himself in' and establish a working relationship with the local gentry. The King was the ruler, but society could only function successfully with co-operation on the part of the ruled.

The key development that gave these noblemen their power (and with it the ability to challenge the Crown on occasion), was the withering of the old landed bond between lord and man and its replacement by the contract, or indenture. The system whereby each landholder undertook to provide the king or his overlord with the services of a fixed number of soldiers as part of his obligation to him had worked well in the years immediately after the Conquest, but as time passed it became increasingly apparent that those who held the land – or owed the landlords their allegiance – were not always the best warriors. The feudal host was last summoned in 1327, but long before this, certainly by 1277 and possibly earlier, kings began to enter into agreements that required lords to bring a certain number of men of proven quality (over and above their feudal commitment) to serve with the royal army for a fixed period, and for which they received an agreed monetary payment. Some peers may have disliked the change – perhaps they felt that accepting money for their services reduced them to the level of mercenary captains – but by the middle of the fourteenth century the contract had become the normal and accepted way of raising armies. The first agreements were simple and possibly oral; but they came to cover such matters as the strength and composition of the contingents to be brought, the period and place of service, the rate of wages and bonus, compensation for lost horses, liability for the costs of transport, and how profits, prisoners' ransoms and captured properties were to be divided between the King and his man.

Not surprisingly, the magnates began to raise their promised contingents in a similar manner, by offering contract engagements to tenants, relatives, members of the county community, and others who wished to take service under them. At first the agreements were purely military in character, but the surviving evidence suggests that quite early, certainly by the second decade of the fourteenth century, the relationships they created were becoming more permanent. Contracts began to include undertakings that one party would 'stay with' the other, in war *and* peace, and for *the term of their two lives*, or at least (in practice) for as long as they thought it mutually advantageous. This is the beginning of what is usually called 'bastard feudalism' – the process whereby a lord's power came to be measured not in terms of the number of tenants bound to his lands but in terms of the quantity and quality of the contract retainers he could summon when needed. These men remained at the Crown's service, but their first loyalty was to the lords who had retained them and they could be used both to overawe local rivals and to emphasise their master's importance at Court.

The retinues were potentially far stronger than the old land-based forces because whereas a lord's following had previously been limited to his tenants and household, there was now theoretically no limit to the number of men he could retain on a short-term basis when danger threatened. Many later contracts required the retainer to bring an agreed number of men to his lord's service or, alternatively, to attend 'accompanied with as many persons defensibly arrayed as he may goodly make and assemble'; and it is easy to see how such forces rapidly became private armies. It has been argued that 'bastard feudalism', far from being a pale shadow of true feudalism, provided a much-needed alternative framework for regulating the relationship between lord and vassal, a relationship that was potentially more stable and enduring because the contracts were entered into freely. The retainers undoubtedly recognised a shared 'community of interest', a bond that bound them to one another as well as to their overlord; but the fly in the ointment was that each lord, as part of his agreement, promised to *maintain* his clients, giving them access to offices and patronage, assisting them in any disputes and difficulties in which they found themselves, and generally looking after their interests as they minded his. There was no harm in this as long as a lord used his influence to help his man obtain a just and reasonable settlement at court, for example; but all too often the retainer's case would be weak and his master secured him a better outcome than he really deserved. Successive governments tried to reform the system by allowing only peers of the realm to recruit followings and prescribing who could, or could not, be engaged by them; but Warwick and his brothers-in-law would have had little difficulty in contracting with those who were willing to fight for them in foreign (and ultimately internal) conflicts, or exercise influence on their behalf in the regions. Edward IV theoretically prohibited all retaining with the exception of household servants, officials and legal advisers; but even he had to allow that the new restrictions should not apply to what was tacitly described as 'lawful service'. The King had no substitute for this unfortunately 'necessary evil', and William, Lord Hastings (our best documented example) signed agreements with many local knights and gentry in the years after 1472.

But perhaps the greatest change – one that affected all classes in fifteenth-century society – was that people were now able to 'better' themselves in ways that would have been unthinkable for most of the Middle Ages. Individuals who possessed special talent had always been able to rise above the scrum and improve their lot in life, but the events of the fourteenth century had allowed a new generation to become 'upwardly mobile' as never before. Men who had bought lands with the profits they earned from trade, from the law, or by taking part in the Hundred Years' War now possessed all the qualifications they needed for higher status except for blood and lineage, while the lower classes had seen their situation transformed by the Black Death. Some peasants who had survived were able to take over the tenements of families who had succumbed to the pestilence, while others ran away and sold their labour to the highest bidder. These comments apply almost exclusively to men since the law actively discriminated against women. Widows enjoyed a reasonable degree of autonomy and some married women were allowed to trade separately from their husbands within the confines of London; but the only way a single girl could improve her lot was to make a good marriage. Women who found well-to-do husbands enhanced their social standing and gained a measure of freedom in the domestic arena, but were still obliged to defer to their spouses in all other matters. There were doubtless instances where wives ruled behind the scenes by sheer force of personality, but they had few rights they could claim for themselves.

Later medieval society can be portrayed as a giant melting-pot – or perhaps a tall ladder would be a more suitable simile – in which everyone was seeking to rise in the world while trying desperately to keep those beneath them in their place! No one ever admitted to this, of course, but we can see it reflected both in the barriers to social mobility that came into existence in the fourteenth and fifteenth centuries, and in laws passed by Parliament to maintain the status quo. By 1450 dukes, marquises and viscounts had joined earls and barons in the ranks of the peerage (allowing for promotion without 'swamping' the established categories), while those with older titles claimed seniority over newcomers within each class. Lower down the scale, a new designation 'gentleman' came into use to accommodate those who were now too wealthy to be described as yeomen, but not rich enough (apparently) to be termed squires, hitherto the lowest aristocratic category. A sumptuary law passed in 1363 had regulated the clothing that could be worn by different social groups (and even what people could eat!), while statutes that prohibited 'butchers, shoemakers, tailors and other low persons' from hunting with dogs and prescribed penalties for those who concocted imaginary coats of arms for themselves all served the same purpose. Such concerns sound prosaic, nonsensical even, to our twenty-first-century ears; but Parliament would not have spent time debating matters that were of no interest to its members, and the point is surely that these things mattered very much to them.

Another indication of the importance that contemporaries attached to their social standing is how frequently men took the opportunity to mention not only their present status but also their previous designations, although those who did so were likely to be on the way up rather than coming back down again! Individual noblemen were, of course, far wealthier and more powerful than any knight, squire or gentleman, but figures compiled by H.L. Grey from tax returns on landed income in 1436 make it very clear that while the fifty-one lay peers had a combined income of £40,000 per annum, the knights and gentry were collectively in receipt of approximately £175,000, over four times as much.[15] Beneath them, yeomen, husbandmen, self-employed craftsmen and small-scale traders were all benefiting from the general rise in living standards, and enjoying an affluence – and precedence – that would have been unthinkable a century earlier. Few noblemen could ignore or resist this combined thrust from the lower reaches of society and the sisters must have recognised that the old certainties that had sustained their families in earlier generations were fast disappearing. It was a new world fraught with difficulties and compounded by the troubles of a civil war.

3

THE SISTERS AND THE WARS
*c.*1450–1461

*C*ecily Neville, the sister nearest in age to Richard of Warwick, died in 1450. Her first husband, Duke Henry, had passed away in 1446 and her second marriage, to John, Lord Tiptoft, who was shortly afterwards created Earl of Worcester, was destined to last for only fifteen months. We do not know what happened to her, although death in or shortly after childbirth is clearly a possibility. Worcester's next wife, Elizabeth Baynham, whom he must have married very soon afterwards, gave birth to a son who died in infancy and was herself dead by April 1452. It is a rather sad reflection on his relationship with Cecily that he subsequently described Elizabeth as 'her … whom I loved best'.[1]

Cecily was laid to rest in the Lady Chapel of Tewkesbury Abbey, the mausoleum of her first husband's Despenser family, but her monument is at Ely Cathedral where she, Worcester and Elizabeth were provided with what have been described as 'wonderfully unsophisticated' stone effigies on a chest beneath a triple canopied tomb in the south choir aisle.[2] Little else of her has come down to us, but there is evidence that she admired fine books and patronised their makers. Worcester owned two that he must have inherited from her, Duke Henry's Psalter and Book of Hours (now Pierpont Morgan Library, New York, MS. M.893), and a handsome copy of John Lydgate's *Fall of Princes* (now Royal MS. 18.D.IV) that bears her arms. She is also mentioned in an inscription requesting prayers for her soul added to a volume described as 'the finest English illuminated manuscript of its time' the so-called 'Hours of Elizabeth the Queen' (British Library Additional MS. 50001).[3] This takes its name from a signature of Elizabeth of York, Henry VII's queen, that appears beneath the miniature of the Crucifixion (figure 22), and although not commissioned by Cecily (it has been dated to *c.*1420–30), could have come into her possession at some time in the 1430s or 1440s. It would have made a magnificent gift when she married her first husband in 1436.

Cecily is the only sister who was indisputably a patroness of literature, but it is probable that her siblings also possessed and read beautiful books. Their grandmother, Joan Beaufort, owned a variety of works including Rolle's *Meditations on the Passion*, *The Chronicle of Jerusalem* and the Arthurian romance *Tristram*, while two of their aunts, Cecily, Duchess of York and Anne, Duchess of Buckingham, have been described as 'significant figures in the history of piety and book-patronage in the fifteenth century'.[4] Archbishop George, their brother, gave valuable books to the universities and employed a scribe to copy the works of Plato; his brother-in-law the Earl of Worcester commissioned and collected numerous volumes in Italy; and Margaret's husband, the Earl of Oxford, possessed a large quantity of mass-books, antiphonals and 'pricke song bokis bounde in leder' among his 'chapel-stuff', together with 'a cheste full of frenshe and englisshe bokes'.[5] Such interests tend to run in families, and the sisters were bound to be influenced by this literary environment. They were born into the old world of handwritten manuscripts, but the printing presses were well established by the time the last of them died.

What did the sisters read or what were they encouraged to read as children and adolescents? The answer is probably much the same material as their brothers since little was written specifically for girls. They would probably have known Geoffrey de la Tour Landry's *Book of the Knight of the Tower*, a work composed in France in the 1370s in which the author used stories culled from a wide range of literature to teach his daughters wisdom and good behaviour; and perhaps the poem *How the Good Wife Taught her Daughter*, although this seems to be aimed more at town-dwellers than young noblewomen. The romance of *Blanchardyn and Eglantine*, which Caxton later considered essential reading for 'gentle young ladies and damsels for to learn to be steadfast and constant',[6] was another favourite, as was *Bevis of Hampton*, which tells of a youth whose father has been murdered by his mother and her unsavoury lover. Bevis and his sweetheart Josian have a number of adventures in the course of his search for justice, and Josian's involvement would have made the story popular among girls. Both sexes enjoyed tales of the legendary deeds of heroes such as Arthur and Jason, and would have been familiar with collections of fables (written by, or based on, Æsop), and with ballads of Robin Hood and other outlaws of the past. The range of books available was obviously limited, but they probably enjoyed them as much as children enjoy stories of larger-than-life characters today.

II

Cecily's death must have cast a cloud over the Neville family, but the silver lining was that her dower third of the Warwick inheritance would now fall to her brother Richard and add to his status as Premier Earl.[7] The future looked promising, but the 1450s were a decade of growing troubles that witnessed the first conflicts of the Wars of the Roses. This is not the place to begin a long discussion of the causes of the Wars, but it would be misleading to place all the blame on Henry VI personally. Long before he was born his grandfather, Henry Bolingbroke, had seized Richard II's throne although he was not the King's heir apparent; and his father, Henry V, had begun a costly and ultimately unwinable war with France. An able king might have survived both an unsuccessful war and a rival claimant, but Henry was a weak man dominated by a court faction that included his French wife, Margaret, and the Dukes of Somerset and Suffolk. Margaret had been married to Henry in 1445 as part of an agreement which, it was hoped, would allow England to retain at least some of his father's French conquests, and the loss of Normandy five years later was a serious blow to national pride. Suffolk, the main architect of the policy, and Somerset, who had latterly commanded in France, were widely blamed for the debacle, but Henry believed that his friends had been implementing policies that enjoyed his approval and was impervious to demands for change.

Change, however, if it could not come by agreement, was destined to come eventually by force. Margaret, Suffolk and Somerset had monopolised the royal patronage and excluded Richard, Duke of York and other noblemen who did not share their opinions from the royal counsels. York, Henry's kinsman and heir-presumptive, had been appointed King's Lieutenant in Ireland in 1447 to prevent him from challenging the Government's policies, but the decision had enhanced his reputation by absolving him of any blame for recent events in Normandy. He needed access to Henry to recover monies owed him for earlier campaigns in France, and following the disturbances of 1450 – Suffolk's murder by an angry mob and Jack Cade's Kentish rebellion – returned to England determined to seize the initiative from his opponents. His problem, as he soon discovered, was that Henry was not legally or constitutionally obliged to give in to demands for reform, even when they were clearly in the national interest. The concept of 'loyal opposition' had not yet been invented, and anyone who confronted the king, who tried to compel him to change his policies, was more likely to be punished as a traitor than rewarded for his concern for the realm.

York was obliged to concede defeat in 1450 – Somerset was briefly sent to the Tower before being restored to favour – but the loss of much of English Gascony in 1451 dealt another blow to the court party. The Duke protested his loyalty to Henry while simultaneously raising an army that would compel the King to change his advisers, but found that the nobility as a whole would not support him. Michael Hicks has pointed out that 'there was an enormous difference between constitutional action in Parliament albeit backed by force and an insurrection that like all rebellions was treasonable',[8] and when York confronted Henry at Dartford (Kent) in 1452 the hopelessness of his position was immediately apparent. He was fortunate that the King had no desire to punish or even humiliate him, and he was allowed to retire to his estates after swearing a formal, public oath of allegiance that he would bear Henry 'feithe and trouthe'.

The Earls of Salisbury and Warwick had supported the King at Dartford and had been duly rewarded; but it was not long before their own relationship with him began to deteriorate. One problem was that the Duke of Somerset was married to the second of Warwick's wife's half-sisters, and the more powerful Somerset became, the greater the likelihood that he and his brother-in-law Shrewsbury would try to deprive Warwick of part of the Beauchamp inheritance. Warwick was perhaps fortunate that in 1452–53 Somerset was preoccupied with the business of government and Shrewsbury in leading the campaign that would end in bloody defeat at Castillon; but another cloud appeared on the horizon when King Henry decided to create his half-brothers Edmund and Jasper (his mother's sons by her Welsh squire Owen Tudor) Earls of Richmond and Pembroke. Edmund was granted the castle, honour, overlordship of feudal tenants and feefarm of Richmond (Yorkshire) that Salisbury had long coveted, and although the latter was appointed to some key offices in the region he was clearly disappointed. A further blow was that the precedence given to the new Tudor earls demoted Warwick to third place in the comital pecking order, and his failure to secure election to the Order of the Garter (after Viscount Bourchier had nominated him on 7 May 1453) undoubtedly rubbed salt in the wound.

These factors probably annoyed the Neville earls without making them active enemies of the Government; and it was another difficulty – their quarrel with the family of Henry Percy, second Earl of Northumberland – that ultimately drove them into York's camp. We do not know when, where or why this dispute began, but there were clearly tensions where their areas of influence overlapped in northern England. This was not in itself unusual since great men were often rivals within particular localities, but the situation worsened after Salisbury's second son, Thomas, was betrothed to Maud Stanhope. The young couple stood to inherit the manor of Wressle which the Crown had confiscated from the Percies in 1405 (Maud was co-heiress of her uncle, Lord Cromwell, the present holder of the property), but Northumberland and his rumbustious son Thomas, Lord Egremont were determined to recover it.[9] Egremont had clearly been threatening his rivals when he was summoned to appear before the royal Council on 8 June 1453, and he was fortunately absent from another Percy manor, Topcliff, when Salisbury's son John attacked it a few weeks later. The two earls were urged to control their offspring, but on 24 August there was an altercation at Heworth, just outside York, between Egremont, allegedly commanding a 5,000-strong army, and a wedding party that included Salisbury, John Neville and the newly married Thomas. This was the incident that the chronicler known as pseudo-Worcester would describe as 'the beginning of the greatest sorrow in England'[10] when he looked back on the Wars in later years.

Relations were now at breaking point and the dispute escalated into a struggle for regional hegemony in northern England involving Warwick, Northumberland and others who had not been present at Heworth. The Government urged both sides to show restraint and tried to appear neutral; but Somerset and other members of the Council inclined towards the Percies, and the Nevilles felt increasingly marginalised. It was the Crown's duty to settle disputes between rival magnates and, more importantly, prevent the emergence of distinctly pro- and anti-court factions; but critically, Henry VI lost his reason in the autumn of 1453. Somerset and his friends tried to conceal the fact for as long as possible, but eventually had to admit that the country was without leadership and allow York to be appointed Protector. The two Neville earls were brought on to the Council and Somerset again sent to the Tower; but both they and York were dismissed and Somerset released when the King regained his sanity in January 1455. Worse still, Queen Margaret had borne a son in October 1453 and York was no longer heir presumptive to the Crown.

The Duke of York had no alternative but to bow to the King's wishes, but with Salisbury and Warwick on his side he was a far more formidable opponent than when he had stood virtually alone. The three of them always protested their personal loyalty to Henry – their only aim, they said, was to reform his government – but their rule had further alienated them from the court faction. The Percies and the Duke of Exeter (another royal cousin descended from one of Henry IV's sisters) had been excluded from the Council while the protectorate lasted and York's departure allowed them to rejoin Somerset at the heart of government. Professor Hicks notes that 'the two Neville earls had committed themselves more than any other magnates to the protectorate and stood to lose most, not least because they had exploited their opportunities to their personal advantage and the disadvantage of others. They could not,' he continues, 'withdraw from politics without repercussions', and had left themselves with no alternative but to resort to force. The King summoned them to meet him at Leicester at the end of May 1455, but when he and his entourage marched out of London they found York and the Nevilles waiting arrayed for battle at St Albans. Negotiations proved fruitless – Henry could not, and would not, give in to demands made by rebels in arms – and were ended when Warwick launched a surprise attack on the royal party. Within two hours the slightly wounded King was a prisoner of the Yorkists, and Somerset, Northumberland and others lay dead in the streets.

The Yorkist lords' victory had destroyed their enemies and put them back in the driving seat, but at a price. They could hardly claim to be the King's loyal subjects when they had risked killing him by shooting arrows (their 'excuse', that they had acted in self-defence, was risible) and their ruthless takeover suggested that they were more interested in benefiting themselves than the country. York became Constable of England, Salisbury was appointed chief steward of the northern parts of the Duchy of Lancaster, Warwick succeeded Somerset as Captain of Calais and George, Salisbury's youngest son, was consecrated Bishop of Exeter, although he was under the minimum canonical age. Their authority was further enhanced when the King's illness recurred in October 1455 and York again became Protector; but this time there were no repercussions when Henry recovered. The King was prepared to allow the Duke to act as chief counsellor, and hoped that everyone shared his desire for peace.

However, it was not to be. The new Duke of Somerset and the new Earl of Northumberland still wanted revenge for their fathers' murders, and Queen Margaret feared that the all-powerful Yorkists would deny her son the succession if the King died. Henry responded by brokering an agreement that required York, Salisbury and Warwick to make reparations to the families of their enemies and threatened all parties with large fines if they failed to keep their promises. There was a formal reconciliation on 25 March 1458 when the protagonists went arm-in-arm to St Paul's, York walking with the Queen, Salisbury with Somerset, and Warwick with Exeter; but the 'Loveday' (as it is known) was undermined by the Yorkist lords' continuing belief that they – and only they – were the arbiters of sound government. It was Warwick, whose impetuousness had started the fight at St Albans, who now rocked the boat by using his position as Captain of Calais to engage in acts of piracy against the ships of both allies and neutrals; and it was perhaps the fear that he and his friends were seeking to shape foreign policy that led to new charges being brought against them in 1459. The King summoned them to attend the next meeting of the great Council and gave them what amounted to a final warning, but they had no intention of obeying orders they believed emanated from the Queen and their other enemies. They again raised forces while protesting their loyalty to Henry personally, but found that few believed – or underestimated – them any longer. An attempt to intercept Salisbury *en route* to join up with York and Warwick was defeated at Blore Heath near Market Drayton, but October found the Yorkist forces effectively hemmed in by the royalists at Ludford Bridge. The difference between this confrontation and St Albans was that the Yorkist lords had been proclaimed traitors in the aftermath of Blore Heath, and any who supported them in these circumstances would be risking everything. They recognised the hopelessness of their position and fled into the night: York to Ireland, and Salisbury and Warwick to Calais.

It may appear strange that the Yorkist lords, having 'cleansed' the Council in 1455, should find themselves in much the same situation four years later, but the fact of the matter is that the only Council ever really acceptable to them was one dominated by themselves. Warwick controlled the seas – a daring raid on Sandwich in which his men captured a number of ships was followed by a visit to York in Ireland to co-ordinate strategy – and the Government could do little but wait for their enemies to return. The two Neville earls and York's eldest son, Edward, Earl of March landed in Kent on 26 June 1460 and gained admission to London. Henry ordered his friends to assemble at Northampton, but not all of them had arrived when Warwick and March reached the town on 10 July. They demanded an audience, and when this was refused mounted an attack on the smaller royal army that cost the lives of the Duke of Buckingham, the Earl of Shrewsbury (son of the earl slain at Castillon) and the ubiquitous Lord Egremont. Henry was captured and again obliged to accept their protestations of loyalty, but all hope of reconciliation with the Queen and her allies was at an end.

The Yorkist lords were now back in charge of the Government, a government dominated increasingly by the dynamic Warwick rather than the ageing Salisbury (who had been left in command of the capital when his son and nephew had marched to Northampton) and the still absent York. The Duke did not return from Ireland until September, and then astounded everyone – his friends as much as his enemies – by claiming that he and not Henry was the rightful king. The merits of York's argument need not detain us,[11] but it was based on a very narrow interpretation of the existing criteria and cut little ice with the lords of the Council. Warwick was angry that he had been kept in the dark and that his claims to be a loyal subject had been made to appear fraudulent;[12] but he eventually formulated a compromise that would allow Henry to reign for the rest of his lifetime if he recognised York as his successor. Compromises need consensus to be successful however, and Queen Margaret refused to accept an arrangement that would deny the throne to her son.

The outcome was that Margaret began to raise forces in northern England, and was joined there by her West Country allies, the Dukes of Somerset and Exeter, and her kinsman the Earl of Devon. The Yorkists agreed that Warwick would remain in London with King Henry while York and Salisbury dealt with the opposition; but the Duke and his brother-in-law found themselves isolated at York's castle of Sandal near Wakefield at the end of December. Details are sketchy, but one of those who enticed or tricked them into offering battle on the 31st may have been John, Lord Neville, younger brother of the second Earl of Westmoreland, who had apparently agreed to support York and his kinsman Salisbury but changed sides at the last moment. York, Salisbury's son Thomas and son-in-law William Bonville, Lord Harrington (Katherine Neville's husband, see below) were slain in the conflict, while Salisbury was captured and lynched by the commons at Pontefract the day after. He was apparently no more popular with ordinary people than with rival members of the northern nobility, but whether this was for partisan, political reasons or because he was regarded as a harsh landlord is unclear.

Margaret and her victorious army now marched southwards and confronted and defeated Warwick at the second battle of St Albans on 17 February 1461. She deprived the Yorkist-dominated government of its legitimacy by regaining possession of her hapless husband, but did not then force her way into London. This allowed the young Earl of March (now titular Duke of York) to enter the capital after joining forces with the remnants of his cousin's army, and they agreed that Warwick would attempt to secure the throne for him. It is ironic that the Earl was willing to make Edward king only five weeks after rejecting his father's bid to supersede Henry, but the loss of royal authority was critical. If Warwick could not rule through Henry of Windsor, he would 'make' a king of his own.

The Queen could not keep her large and apparently poorly disciplined army in the field indefinitely, and was eventually obliged to retreat northwards. Warwick, Edward (who had been proclaimed Edward IV on 3 March) and their friends set off in pursuit of them, and won a decisive victory at Towton (Yorkshire) on Palm Sunday. Margaret and Henry found refuge in Scotland (they surrendered Berwick and were prepared to return Calais to the French in return for aid as and when they recovered it), but resistance to the Yorkists in England was thereafter confined largely to the great Northumbrian castles of Alnwick, Bamburgh and Dunstanburgh. These finally surrendered in 1464 after Warwick's brother John had destroyed small Lancastrian armies at Hedgeley Moor and Hexham; and when Henry was captured shortly afterwards Margaret and her son sought safety in France. Only Harlech, in Wales, held out for them until 1468.

III

Salisbury used the uneasy years of the 1450s to conclude the marriages of several of his younger children. Thomas, his second son, was (as we have noted) married to Maud Stanhope in 1453, while John, his third son, wed Isabel Ingoldsthorpe, who had a residual claim to the earldom of Worcester, in April 1457. Eleanor was joined to Thomas, son and heir of Lord Stanley of Lathom (Lancashire), Alice espoused her father's associate Henry, Lord Fitzhugh of Ravensworth (Yorkshire), while Katherine was contracted to William Bonville who was sixteen when his right to succeed his maternal grandfather's barony of Harrington was recognised in 1458.[13] They were all members of solid, baronial families, but poorer and less influential than the earls Salisbury had secured for his two elder daughters in the 1430s. He would have preferred to arrange great, as opposed to acceptable, matches for all his offspring, to have dealt in certainties rather than in potential benefits; but opportunities were inevitably limited and his ability to secure them may have diminished as the years passed. His mother's death in 1440 broke his direct link with the royal family (the reigning king, Henry VI, was only his second cousin of the half blood) and he lost another powerful ally when Cardinal Henry Beaufort, his mother's wealthy and influential brother, died in 1447. Beaufort had helped Salisbury secure his favourable settlement with the elder Nevilles, and had earlier brokered an agreement stipulating how any Montacute lands recovered in France would be divided between his nephew and the Countess Alice's stepmother's new husband. Mother and uncle were irreplaceable, and as Salisbury's own influence declined powerful men did not always seek his friendship as they had his father's a generation earlier. He attended only three of fifty-seven meetings of the Council held between 1447 and 1449, and Professor Griffiths suggests that it was noblemen, who might aspire to succeed if Henry died childless, who were courted after 1438.[14]

We do not, unfortunately, possess details of any of the marital arrangements that Salisbury made for his younger children, but they would have incorporated a number of provisions designed to protect the young couples' interests. Usually, the bride's father would give the groom's father a dowry (not to be confused with a widow's *dower*) and the groom's father would settle lands on his son and new daughter-in-law in jointure.[15] These would provide the children with an independent income and would continue to be held by the wife if her husband died early – an important consideration if he had not inherited his father's properties. It would probably be agreed that the girl would move in with her in-laws until the young couple were old enough to have their own establishment on one of the groom's father's subsidiary estates.

The age at which a young bride and groom were to be allowed to cohabit would also have been central to the contract. Sexual relations often began early – Margaret Beaufort gave birth to the future Henry VII when she was only thirteen and Elizabeth Woodville was delivered of her eldest son by her first husband at a similar age[16] – but the evidence suggests that Salisbury and his countess were genuinely concerned for their daughters' welfare. Their four younger girls were wedded in their late teens or early twenties and began to bear their children almost immediately; but their two elder sisters, who were significantly younger when they married, did not start their families until they reached maturity. Joan was married to the Earl of Arundel in 1438 when she was about fourteen, but her eldest son was not born until 1450; and although Cecily was joined to Henry, Lord Despenser, her first husband, at the tender age of nine, she did not have her first child until nine years later. Salisbury himself had wed Alice Montacute in 1421 when he would have been about twenty-one and she approximately fifteen; but it was three years before she gave birth to the first of their many offspring. Business contracts (for that is what they were) did not have to be devoid of humanity and all six daughters may have been grateful to their parents in this respect.

The girls' marriages effectively released them from their father's authority, but placed them entirely in the hands of their husbands. They had no separate legal existence, were expected to behave demurely and obediently, and would be severely punished for any shortcomings. Husbands routinely beat their wives 'violently, with whips and sticks', because they genuinely thought it was good for them, and because it seemed the best way of restraining their supposed tendency towards 'foolish and loose' behaviour! They could act independently on occasion however, and were very much their husbands' partners in the sense that they identified themselves with all their interests. In the frequent absences of the elder John Paston, it was his wife, Margaret, who, besides managing the household, took his place at the head of the family and shouldered any and every responsibility. Warwick's sisters had even larger estates to concern them, and a multiplicity of servants to command and control.

None of the sisters were ever separated, or divorced, from their husbands, but this does not mean that their marriages were all blissfully happy. It was almost impossible to obtain a divorce in the Middle Ages, although a couple might seek an *annulment* on the grounds that their union was invalid for one of a number of reasons. An unhappily married lady could 'discover' that she was related to her husband within the fourth degree of consanguinity or affinity, argue that one of them had been pre-contracted to another person at the time of their marriage, or plead that she had been married under age. These would be matters for a church court to decide, as would any claim for an annulment based on the husband's alleged impotence, or crime, for example if a woman believed that her spouse was planning to kill her. She would lose her right to dower in the event of her husband's death, of course, and there could be repercussions from within her own family. She might take the risk if she was a considerable landowner in her own right or had another man ready and waiting to marry her, but it was a brave lady who defied the conventions to take responsibility for her own life.

Warwick's sisters were not themselves great heiresses and would have had to resign themselves to whatever hand fate dealt them, but there is no evidence that any of their husbands treated them badly. William, Lord Hastings was a notorious philanderer, but Katherine, his wife, seems to have accepted this much as Elizabeth Woodville tolerated the 'privy pleasures'[17] King Edward shared with him. He could still refer to her as 'Kateryn myn entyerly beloved wyffe'[18] when he appointed her his executor in 1482, and two wills made by her sisters' husbands express similar sentiments. Thomas, Lord Stanley asked to be buried with Eleanor, his first wife, at Burscough priory (Lancashire) although she had predeceased him by thirty-two years, and John de Vere, Earl of Oxford chose to lie 'tofore the highe aulter of our Lady Chapell in the Priory of Colne in the Countie of Essex in a tombe whiche I have made and ordeyned for me and Margaret my late wif where she nowe lieth buried'.[19] Both men had subsequently remarried – Stanley had wed Margaret Beaufort and Oxford had espoused Elizabeth Scrope, widow of his old friend Viscount Beaumont – but both surely felt genuine affection for their first partners. They may have been no more than acquaintances at the outset, but years of sharing – and a sense of 'duty' – had made their unions work.

Lord Hastings is the only one of the sisters' husbands who is known to have engaged in extramarital relationships, but it would be remarkable if his seven brothers-in-law were all paragons of virtue. Attitudes to infidelity have varied considerably over the centuries and medieval ladies seem to have been generally tolerant of this aspect of their marriages because the concubines posed little or no threat to their positions as wives and mistresses of their households. A fifteenth-century nobleman would, as we have noted, found it all but impossible to divorce his wife in order to marry his concubine, and wives who had married for political or other reasons may not have felt cheated if their relationships with their husbands remained purely formal. Some clandestine affairs almost certainly resulted in the birth of illegitimate children but, again, there is no trace of them in the record. Warwick had an illegitimate daughter named Margaret whom he married to Richard, son of Sir John Huddleston of Millom (Cumbria), while his uncle Fauconberg had at least two such sons (Thomas, the 'Bastard of Fauconberg', and William); but even Lord Hastings did not, so far as is known, acknowledge or provide for illicit offspring in his lifetime or leave them anything in his will. It is, of course, possible that illegitimate children were born to some of these noblemen, but that none lived to grow up. Geoffrey de la Tour Landry counselled his daughters to fast three or four days a week to subdue the flesh, but it would be surprising if they − or other young noblewomen − heeded his advice!

4

THE SISTERS IN THE FIRST REIGN OF EDWARD IV

he loss of their father and second brother at Wakefield was clearly a major blow for all the sisters, but it was Katherine, whose husband and father-in-law fell in the same battle, who was perhaps most bruised by this phase of the conflict. Her daughter, Cecily, may have been born posthumously and she would have expected a smaller widow's portion than if Lord Harrington had lived to inherit his grandfather's Bonville manors. Cecily was heiress to both baronies by the time Edward IV became king, and many years of defending the child's rights against predators stretched before her; but few would have dared threaten her after she wed the King's friend William, Lord Hastings only months later. There can be little doubt that Warwick arranged this marriage for his sister, a marriage that provided her with wealth and security for most of the reign.[1]

In theory, a widow could choose her own second husband, but family pressures and individual circumstances meant that this was not always possible. Girls and younger women still had the potential to add to the family's acres, while dowagers who remarried could alienate property their sons had expected to inherit. It is no coincidence that Katherine and Cecily, who were both widowed early, remarried, while Alice remained single for over thirty years after Lord Fitzhugh died in 1472. Katherine did not marry for a third time after Lord Hastings was executed eleven years later, again, possibly, because the custom of the courtesy of England would have allowed her new spouse to continue to hold her estates after her death. She and Alice would both have attracted the attentions of younger, impoverished suitors, but the decisions were not always theirs to make.

II

Katherine's wedding to Lord Hastings would have been a happy family occasion, but there would have been more sadness for the sisters when Joan died shortly before 9 September 1462. Again, we know nothing of the circumstances, but her passing seems to have profoundly affected the Earl of Arundel, her husband for twenty-four years. He never remarried, although he lived on for another quarter of a century, and thereafter played little part in national politics. He had been indicted after the rout at Ludlow in 1459 and had fought with Warwick, his brother-in-law, at second St Albans and Towton; but his involvement in the troubles of 1469–71 seems to have been limited to accompanying the King into Kent after the battle of Tewkesbury, and he did not go to France with Edward in 1475.[2] It could be argued that he would have been fifty-two by 1469–70 and too old for soldiering; but John Howard, Duke of Norfolk was over sixty when he was killed at the battle of Bosworth, and Howard's son, Thomas, was aged about seventy when he defeated the Scots at Flodden in 1513. There can be little doubt that Arundel chose to lead a quiet, largely rural, existence, a decision that may, or may not, have been forced upon him by injury or worsening health problems. We can only say that he seems to have been close to Warwick in what may be called the first War of the Roses, but apparently distanced himself from him after Joan's death.

III

Another matter that ultimately threatened family unity – although no one at the time would have appreciated it – was the trial and execution of the twelfth Earl of Oxford and his eldest son, Aubrey, by Cecily's widower, John Tiptoft, Earl of Worcester. Worcester was a career politician who studied at Oxford University in the early 1440s and progressed to become Treasurer of England in 1452 and joint keeper of the seas two years later. He does not seem to have been present at the first battle of St Albans, and left England early in 1458 to study and indulge his passion for book collecting in Italy. His long absence meant that he played no part in the troubles of 1459–61 that culminated in the deposition of King Henry, but he was summoned home soon after Edward IV's accession and appointed Constable of England on 7 February 1462. The terms of his new office allowed him to try cases of treason on simple inspection of fact (without a jury), and he acquired a reputation for ruthlessness that soon matched his renown as a scholar. We do not know if any of those he summarily sentenced to be beheaded asked him for mercy, but they would almost certainly have asked in vain.

The Earl of Oxford had continued to conspire with other disaffected Lancastrians after Edward IV's accession, and was arrested, together with his eldest son and several associates, five days before Worcester was appointed Constable. The 'hyghe and mighty treson that [he] ymagened agayne the Kynge'[3] brought him to the scaffold on 26 February, where his head was 'smyten of, that alle menne myght see, whereof the moste peple were sory'.[4] Oxford was fifty-three – again, rather elderly by the standards of the time – and had been excused from attending both Council and Parliament because of ill health as recently as November 1460; but it may have been more than this that earned him the sympathy of the onlookers. The contemporary writer John Warkworth believed that Worcester had judged him 'by lawe padowe' (by the law of Padua),[5] and there was an element of revulsion that foreign (and therefore unacceptable) concepts the Earl had learned in Italy were being used against Englishmen in their own land.

Oxford's eldest son and most of the others followed him to the block six days later, but the family was not attainted and John, his next heir, succeeded to the title in 1464. Edward IV was anxious to conciliate him, and his marriage to Margaret, Warwick's youngest sister, in the mid-1460s was probably part of this process; but John had no love for Worcester or the king who employed him. He was sent to the Tower after becoming embroiled in a new Lancastrian conspiracy in 1468, but saved his neck by confessing 'myche thinges'[6] and was pardoned on 15 April 1469. His persistent loyalty to the House of Lancaster was, as we shall see, destined to cause Margaret much financial as well as political difficulty, and he may have been somewhat impecunious at the best of times. A letter he wrote to Sir John Paston towards the end of the decade asked Paston 'to ordeyne me iij. horsse harneys as godely as ye and Genyn kan devyse, as it were for yourselfe'. He was prepared to pay £6 or £7 each for them, but it was Margaret who was to find the money – 'and my wife shalle deliver you silver, – and yit she most borowed it'![7] Oxford – like some modern aristocrats – had wealth tied up in land and property, but clearly sometimes lacked ready cash!

IV

The Earl of Arundel's estrangement from the Nevilles would explain why, surprisingly, he was absent from both the Earl of Salisbury's reburial at Bisham Priory in February 1463 and the banquet held at Cawood Castle after George Neville's enthronement as Archbishop of York in September 1465. Salisbury and his son Sir Thomas had been buried at Pontefract after the disaster of Wakefield, and more than two years elapsed before they were re-interred with their ancestors and with the Countess Alice who had died in 1461. Arrangements were made for the bodies to be exhumed and brought southwards, a journey that is entirely lost to us but which would have had many parallels with Edward IV's reburial of *his* father and brother at Fotheringhay thirteen years later. On this occasion the bodies were taken up and placed in coffins on hearses, elaborate roofed structures decorated with heraldic and religious symbols and surrounded by candles. The funeral procession was headed by Richard, Duke of Gloucester, the late Duke of York's youngest son, accompanied by other peers, bishops and abbots, a number of kings of arms, heralds and pursuivants, and 400 poor men carrying large torches dressed in black. The coffins were borne on two carriages draped with black velvet, and York's was pulled by seven horses, again trapped to the ground in black. The churches in the towns through which the cortège would pass had been prepared to receive it (the clergy apparently rode ahead to ensure that all was in readiness) and it was formally received by members of the local guilds and religious orders and watched over by sixty men with torches at night. At each place dirge (or matins) was said shortly after midnight followed by requiem mass before departure, and alms were distributed to the poor.

The chief mourners at Salisbury's elaborate funeral ceremony included Warwick and his brothers, all four of their surviving sisters, two of their three husbands, and their former brother-in-law the Earl of Worcester.[8] The late Earl's surviving brothers, Lords Latimer and Bergavenny were apparently absent (Lord Latimer was still incapacitated and their brother Lord Fauconberg, who had recently been created Earl of Kent, had died on 9 January) and Lord Stanley may have been detained in the north by the need to guard against threats from the Lancastrians and Scots.[9] We know more about these final obsequies than about the journey that preceded them because the heralds who acted as masters of ceremonies kept detailed records of precedent and protocol, both for their own benefit and to assist those who would have to marshal similar events in the future. Warwick, his brother John (now Lord Montagu) and their cousin, Lord Latimer's son Henry 'with many other lords and knights one [on] everie side to the number of fifteen' joined the cortège on Monday 14 February and escorted it to the priory where it was received by Bishop George Neville and other clergy. The black-draped hearse was brought into the choir and placed near the Countess's white covered catafalque attended by her four daughters, her daughter-in-law Joan Ingoldsthorpe, 'and many other ladies and gentewomen'.[10] The King was represented by his brother, the Duke of Clarence and his sister, the Duchess of Suffolk, the deceased's nephew and niece.

Garter and Clarenceux kings of arms and Windsor and Chester heralds stood at the four corners of the Earl's hearse dressed in his livery throughout the service of dirge, and resumed their duties at mass the next morning. Warwick offered his mass-penny, and was then formally presented with his late father's coat of arms, shield, sword, helmet and crest. The coat of arms was brought to him by Garter and the Earl of Worcester, the shield by Clarenceux and John Neville, the sword by Windsor and Lord Hastings, and the helm and crest by Chester and Lord Fitzhugh. Bishop George stood at his side in what was essentially a political, spiritual and not least familial endorsement of his right to inherit, and his sisters watched with pride tinged with sadness as he received the achievements and returned them to the king of arms or herald. The offertory concluded with monetary gifts that reflected the rank of each donor, and with the presentation of embroidered cloths of 'gould bawdken' (oriental silk) that would have been laid on the hearse or coffin in strict order of precedence. Each baron gave one, the Earl of Worcester two, the Duke of Suffolk (who was present with his wife) three, and the Duke of Clarence four.

After the 'gospell of the Masse' (before the offertory), 'the twoe Kinges of Armes went foorth to the west doore of the church whereat there was a man arrede one [on] horsbacke trapped with an axe in his hand with the poynt downwarde. The sayd Kinge receivinge hime into the Quier doore where he allighted, houldinge the sayd horse trapped in hand, in the arms of the sayd earle.' The horseman waited until Warwick had been presented with the achievements, and then 'the residue of herrolds and pursuivantes cominge before the man of armes and the horse trapped, the sayd man of armes convayed betweene twoe barrons was by them presented and offered his armes and horse to the churche; and afterwards was convaighed throughe the church to the revestrie [vestry], there receaved and the man unarmed'.[11]

The achievements were positioned about the tomb prior to the burial, and this done the kings of arms and heralds removed their jackets of the late Earl's livery and collected their fees. There is no record of the feast, or wake, that would have concluded the occasion, but we may suppose that the many guests who stayed at the priory were well refreshed afterwards. The sisters may well have lingered for some days before setting out on their homeward journeys and would have welcomed the opportunity to spend time together and tell each other their 'news'.

It is likely that some – perhaps all – of the senior members of the Neville family were invited to attend the Queen's coronation in May 1465, and we know that they again came together in September when Bishop George was enthroned as Archbishop of York. The ceremony in the Minster is entirely lost to us, but John Leland found 'an old paper roll' that described the feast that followed, how it was ordered, and the vast number of comestibles provided for the guests.[12] Warwick acted as steward for the occasion, his bother John was treasurer, Lord Hastings was controller, and over 2,000 people dined on hundreds of oxen, sheep, pigs, deer, pike, partridges, chickens and pigeons, as well as more exotic creatures such as swans, bitterns, lapwings, curlews, herons, peacocks, porpoises and seals.[13] These were followed by an abundance of jellies, tarts and custards, all washed down with 300 tuns of ale and 100 tuns of wine. It was, as Paul Murray Kendall commented, 'the most famous banquet of fifteenth century England' and 'a lively reminder of the undiminished puissance of the House of Neville'.[14]

No one room could accommodate this many people, so the principal diners sat down to eat in the main hall and in three chambers designated 'chief', 'second' and 'great', while others (the less 'important' people and servants) were packed into the lower hall and gallery. The Earls of Worcester and Oxford sat together at the high table in the hall in what may have been a formal gesture of reconciliation, while Lords Stanley and Fitzhugh were placed with the Earl of Westmoreland and ten barons at the second table in the second chamber. Alice and Katherine had places at the first table in this room, where they were joined by Warwick's countess, Anne Beauchamp, the Dowager Duchess of Suffolk (Alice Chaucer, wife of the duke murdered in 1450), and the 'Countess of Oxford', presumably Margaret if she was married to the Earl by this date. The only sister not, apparently, present was Eleanor, Lady Stanley. She could have been among the baronesses and ladies not identified by the writer; but she was bearing her children in the 1460s and it would not be surprising if she was in the later stages of pregnancy or had recently given birth.

V

Edward IV was now seated securely on his throne and Warwick was at his elbow counselling and guiding, but relations between them deteriorated as the years passed. In May 1464 the King secretly wed an English gentlewoman, Elizabeth Woodville, whose five brothers and seven sisters all had to be given appropriate status or found husbands from among the ranks of the higher nobility. Warwick felt he had been made to appear foolish – his envoys had been seeking to arrange a French marriage for a king who, unbeknown to them, was no longer a bachelor – and he was further aggrieved when some of the nuptials arranged for the new Queen's relatives affected members of his own family. The young Duke of Buckingham, whom he had regarded as a likely husband for his daughter Isabel, was married to Catherine Woodville, the Queen's sister; the heiress of the Duke of Exeter was wed to Elizabeth's elder son by her first marriage instead of to John Neville's son George, his nephew; and his elderly aunt, Katherine, Dowager Duchess of Norfolk, who was in her sixties, was espoused to Elizabeth's brother John Woodville, a young man of about twenty! The Nevilles had received their own share of rewards – Warwick obtained lands, offices and wardships, his brother John had recently been created Earl of Northumberland, and Archbishop George had been Chancellor since 1460 – but it must have been hard for the 'Kingmaker' to accept that men who had fought for Lancaster while he had sustained the Yorkist war effort now rivalled him in Edward's affections. Matters deteriorated further when Edward deprived George of the Great Seal in 1467, and the following year married his sister Margaret to Charles, Duke of Burgundy, the King of France's bitter rival, notwithstanding Warwick's preference for a French alliance. All might have been forgiven if the King had been willing to allow Isabel Neville to marry George, Duke of Clarence, his younger brother, but Edward vetoed this too.

VI

Cecily, Warwick's second sister, and Margaret, the youngest, each had one child: Cecily a daughter who predeceased her and Margaret a son, George, who was living in 1478 but who is said to have died in the Tower during his father's exile.[15] The others were more prolific, Joan bearing at least five children, Eleanor seven, Katherine five, and Alice no fewer than eleven. Joan had four sons, the best known being Thomas, Lord Maltravers (b. c.1450), who succeeded his father as Earl of Arundel, while Eleanor's six boys included George, (b. c.1460), who became Lord Strange in right of his wife, Edward, the first Lord Monteagle, and James, sometime Bishop of Ely.[16] Katherine, who was already the mother of Cecily (Bonville) when she wed Lord Hastings, subsequently produced four sons, Edward (b. 1467), Richard, George and William, and a second daughter, while Alice presented her husband Lord Fitzhugh with six sons, his heir Richard (b. c.1458), Henry, Thomas, John, George and Edward, together with five daughters, Elizabeth, Alice, Beatrix (or Joan), Anne and Margaret (or Margery).[17] The list is almost certainly incomplete – half of all babies born died in their first year of life and a quarter of the survivors before they were fifteen – but we are only concerned here with those who grew up.

A great deal of care and thought would have been lavished on these children, partly because they represented the family's future and because of their value in forging links with other, preferably greater, houses. Joan's son, Thomas, married Queen Elizabeth Woodville's sister Margaret, while Lord Stanley secured the Queen's niece and heiress to the barony of Strange of Knockyn for his eldest son by Eleanor, George. The Kingmaker agreed to join his ward Francis Lovel, the heir to five baronies, to Lord Fitzhugh and Alice's daughter Anne, while Lord Hastings ensured that his ward, George Talbot, Earl of Shrewsbury, became the husband of his (and Katherine's) daughter, another Anne. Hastings's eldest son Edward was joined to Lady Mary Hungerford, heiress to the baronies of Botreux, Moleyns and Hungerford, and his step-daughter Cecily wed the Marquess of Dorset, the Queen's eldest son by her first marriage; but there were no more great weddings after Warwick was killed in 1471 and Hastings executed in 1483. Richard Fitzhugh, Alice's eldest surviving son, had to content himself with the daughter of a prominent knight, Sir Thomas Borough,[18] and Hastings's younger sons, Richard and William, may have been unmarried as late as 1503.

These weddings meant that three of the Kingmaker's sisters' offspring had been married into the extended royal family by 1475 (the year in which Cecily Bonville wed the Marquess of Dorset), the large family of Queen Elizabeth Woodville having provided the groom or bride in each instance. The arrangements were mutually beneficial in the sense that the King wanted to assure himself of the loyalty of these magnates and their connections as much as they wished to benefit from his patronage, but he may also have been using his wife's family to forge links that were his rather than Warwick's. He may have thought that a marriage between Thomas Fitzalan and Margaret Woodville would help to mollify the Earl of Arundel, while the powerful but equivocal Lord Stanley needed to be bound to the new dynasty by any means possible. This was not true of William, Lord Hastings, whose loyalty was always unimpeachable; and it may have been Hastings's own differences with Elizabeth and her family that prompted the marriage of her son to his step-daughter. The sisters were themselves the King's first cousins – their father, Salisbury, was Edward's mother's eldest brother – but this relationship could not guarantee that their offspring would always identify with his family. They needed bonds that were essentially their own.

The careers of some of these children will feature in later chapters of this book, but it is worth pausing here to notice the somewhat notorious reputation of the sons that Eleanor bore Lord Stanley. We know the names of only three of them – the others probably died in infancy – but George, Edward and James are among the most unusual personalities of the time. George is the young man who was held hostage for his father's good behaviour before the battle of Bosworth, and narrowly escaped being executed when it became apparent that Lord Thomas did not intend to support King Richard. He is said to have been poisoned 'at an ungodly banquet' during his father's lifetime, a fate his brother Edward allegedly inflicted on a young man named John Harrington, whose father, Sir James, had been attainted after Bosworth. Edward Stanley had been granted some of Sir James's forfeited properties, and Elizabeth Harrington (John's cousin) subsequently alleged that John had been eliminated to prevent him from seeking to be restored to them. The two families were old enemies[19] and Elizabeth believed that Edward had destroyed his rival to protect his gains.

Edward was created Baron Monteagle and admitted to the Order of the Garter after distinguishing himself at the battle of Flodden, but both he and his younger brother James, who became successively Warden of the

Collegiate Church of Manchester (1485), Dean of St Martin-le-Grand, London, and Bishop of Ely (1506) had a darker side to their characters. Edward was 'believed to be a devil-raiser and alchemist' according to Hampton,[20] while James, who may have owed his promotion at Ely to his step-mother, Margaret Beaufort, led a notably secular lifestyle. Fuller says that he was 'a man more memorable than commendable, who never resided at his own Cathedral. I can partly excuse his living all the summer with the Earl his brother [sic], in this county [Lancashire], but must condemn his living all the winter at his manor at Somersham in Huntingdonshire with one who was not his sister, and wanted nothing to make her his wife save marriage.'[21]

We do not know if the Stanley boys inherited these unfortunate traits from their parents, but if they did it is more likely to have been from their feisty mother Eleanor than from their altogether more cautious father, Lord Thomas. Two letters written by Eleanor (or *Alianour*, to use the contemporary idiom) have survived from this decade and leave little doubt that she was a forceful personality who expected her correspondents to obey her instructions. The first, written on 1 May 1466, concerned a dispute that had arisen between two squires, William Flemmyng and Hugh Brethyrton, over the ownership of some lands and tenements at Longton in Lancashire. Flemmyng and Brethyrton had agreed that Eleanor should appoint an 'indifferent' (neutral) person to collect the rents and farms until they were able to agree a solution, and she named one Richard Banastre as 'overseer and ruler' for the time being.[22]

In the second letter dated 27 August (unfortunately, the year is not stated), Eleanor is found writing to a Piers of Werburton on behalf of an exchequer official named Geffrey Harper. Harper was entitled to an annuity of six marks 'by yere by patent of the lorde of Bergavenny' (Edward Neville, Eleanor's uncle), charged on the lordships of Bromfield and Yale; but the 'baillyfe and occupiers' had 'keped [this] from hym wrongfully', and he asked Eleanor to intercede. Her letter to Werburton asks him to 'tenderly consydre and shewe youre gode will and favor to the said Geffrey and helpe hym to his payement by the nerest meane that ye can', but leaves him in no doubt that his assistance in the matter 'shall cause me to be yo[u]r gode lady'.[23] The implication is that she would *not* be his good lady if he failed to help Harper, and Werburton almost certainly did what he could!

These were problems that could have been brought to the attention of Lord Stanley and his council, but the petitioners had clearly decided to approach Eleanor rather than her husband. This may have been because Stanley was often absent or because the parties feared they were beneath his attention; but there can be no doubt that they believed that Eleanor would give them a fair hearing, and that she could, if she chose, impose a just settlement or persuade others to do her bidding. People traditionally approached the Queen, rather than the King, because they thought she would be more sympathetic to their requests than her husband, and the wives of great noblemen could expect to be asked to consider matters that concerned their own people or localities. Eleanor's sisters would have fulfilled this role just as she did, and, like Queen Elizabeth, would have used their special relationship with their husbands to help find equitable solutions. They may even have persuaded them to change their minds!

Eleanor clearly enjoyed the confidence of a number of persons who looked to the Stanleys for assistance, and was also, apparently, held in some regard by the King. There is no suggestion that she was one of Edward IV's 'conquests', but on 6 April 1464 he gave her 'the mills of Llanvas and Kennecogh within the king's lordship of Bewemares sometime in the tenure of Thomas Nesse and William Cranwell, with the demesne rents of all lands and tenements sometime of Richard Kyghley within the said lordship, which used to render 4l 14s 4d as appears in the court rolls of the lordship, rendering yearly a red rose at Midsummer'.[24] Edward was desperately short of money in 1464 – the continuing Lancastrian opposition was placing considerable strain on his resources – and the grant presupposes that he had been impressed by Eleanor's personality and felt obligated to her for some reason. Perhaps he had stayed with her and her husband during one of his earlier campaigns in the north?

VII

Edward was king of course, and fully entitled to make his own decisions for his own reasons; but Warwick felt he had been badly treated by 1469. There was no constitutional outlet for his disappointment – we have already noted that the concept of 'loyal opposition' still lay in the future – and his thoughts turned to finding ways of making Edward appreciate that he could not rule successfully without him. His task was made easier by the fact that there was widespread dissatisfaction with Edward's government by the end of the decade – high taxation and lawlessness remained as prevalent as in Henry VI's reign – and the discontented were only too ready to make their feelings known.

5

THE SISTERS AND THE WARS
1469–1471

*T*here was trouble in Yorkshire in the late spring of 1469, and a captain calling himself 'Robin of Redesdale' (who was probably a member of the Conyers family, related to Warwick by marriage) led a more serious uprising in June. Edward ordered two of his court favourites, William Herbert, the Yorkist Earl of Pembroke, and Humphrey Stafford, now Earl of Devon, to deal with the rebels, but they were decisively defeated at Edgecote, near Banbury, on 24 July. Warwick had married Isabel to Clarence in defiance of the King's wishes thirteen days earlier and in the aftermath of the battle executed Pembroke, the Queen's father Earl Rivers and her brother John. There was no justification for this since both factions, Neville and Woodville, regarded King Edward as their rightful sovereign; but Warwick had decided that merely removing his rivals from the Council board was no longer sufficient. Edward was taken into custody by Archbishop George Neville at Olney in Buckinghamshire, and transferred first to Warwick Castle and then to Middleham. He was now Warwick's prisoner much as Henry VI had once been, but if the Earl thought he could rule through him he was badly mistaken. Few, it appears, would obey orders that did not emanate from Edward personally, and with the situation deteriorating Warwick bowed to the inevitable and allowed him to return to London. It was one thing to rule a Lancastrian king with Yorkist backing, but quite another to dominate a Yorkist monarch virtually alone.

King Edward could now have held Warwick and his new son-in-law Clarence to account for their recent actions, but instead tried to heal the rift that had developed between them. 'The Kyng hymselffe hathe good langage of the Lords of Clarance, of Warwyk ... seying they be hys best frendys'[1] wrote Sir John Paston laconically, an opinion that can hardly have been shared by Queen Elizabeth and others still mourning the losses their families had suffered. Edward went so far as to create the Earl's nephew George, Duke of Bedford, and betroth him to his eldest daughter, Princess Elizabeth; but even the prospect of a close relative joining the royal family could not disguise the fact that Warwick had failed to make his erstwhile protégé obey him or alter the status quo at court. Still disappointed, his thoughts turned to promoting a second, more decisive rebellion and a dispute in Lincolnshire between the Yorkist Sir Thomas Burgh of Gainsborough, and Richard, Lord Welles, the old Lancastrian leader of the county, gave him his opportunity. Word was spread that the King intended to punish large numbers of the commons for supporting Robin of Redesdale's uprising, and before long the shire was up in arms against him. At first, Edward did not suspect that Warwick and Clarence were involved in the revolt and even commissioned them to array troops to help suppress it; but the Lancastrian army advanced into battle at Losecote Field on 12 March 1470 shouting '*A Clarence! a Clarence! a Warrewike*',[2] and their defeated leaders admitted that they had intended to make Clarence king. Warwick knew that there could be no excuses or forgiveness this time, and joined his son-in-law in seeking safety in France.

Their arrival gave King Louis XI a heaven-sent opportunity to make trouble for his brother of England, and at Angers on 22 July he brought Warwick face to face with his old enemy Queen Margaret and persuaded them to overlook their differences. Their new found amity was sealed by the marriage of the Earl's younger daughter Anne to Margaret's son Prince Edward, and it was agreed that Warwick would invade England on behalf of the House of Lancaster and restore the imprisoned King Henry to the throne. Edward believed he had the means and the resources to deal with the renewed threat to his authority, but there was one, potentially fatal, flaw in his armoury. In March of that year he had deprived Warwick's impeccably loyal brother John Neville of the princely earldom of Northumberland in order to restore the Percy heir to his ancestral title. John was compensated with the marquisate of Montagu and by the rewards bestowed on his son George; but was heard to declare that he had been given only 'a pyes [magpie's] neste'[3] with which to maintain his new dignity. The result was that he supported his brother's invasion, and Edward, his army disintegrating, sought refuge in Burgundy with a few loyal friends.

A somewhat bemused Henry VI was brought out of the Tower and restored to the throne he had last occupied nine years earlier, but few could have doubted that it was Warwick who ruled. King Edward was bound to attempt to reverse the situation, and with a small flotilla provided by Duke Charles, his brother-in-law, landed at Ravenspur on the Humber on 14 March 1471. The Neville and Lancastrian forces stationed in northern England should have dealt with his small army without difficulty; but Henry Percy chose not to move against the man who had so recently restored him to his earldom, and John Neville may have had similar qualms of conscience. Edward marched south gathering soldiers, and near Banbury was formally reconciled to his brother Clarence. The Duke's hopes of becoming king had all but disappeared when Warwick threw in his lot with King Henry and Queen Margaret, and there was the added danger that some of his estates would be restored to their former Lancastrian owners when Margaret and her son returned to England. Warwick shut himself up in Coventry to await reinforcements, and Edward entered London on 11 April after Archbishop Neville had failed to organise effective resistance. The crucial battle fought at Barnet three days later culminated in the deaths of both Warwick and Montagu and the total defeat of their army. The Earl, it is said, tried to escape on horseback but was trapped in a wood and slain by his pursuers. It was an undignified end to a remarkable political and military career.

Queen Margaret and her son landed in England on the very day that Warwick fell at Barnet and although her friends raised a new army for her in the West Country it proved too little, too late. The death of the Lancastrian

Prince Edward at Tewkesbury on 4 May and the mysterious demise of his father, King Henry, when the victorious Yorkist army returned to London effectively removed the last serious opposition to King Edward, and brought what may be regarded as the most dramatic twenty-five months in English medieval history to a conclusion.

The bodies of Warwick and Montagu were brought to the capital and displayed on the pavement of St Paul's for three days (to firmly nail any rumours that they had survived Barnet), before Archbishop George was allowed to bury them in Bisham Priory. No record survives of the ceremony, but it must have been a far cry from the magnificent re-interment of their father in the same place only eight years previously. The only mourners of any consequence were probably Archbishop George and – if King Edward had sufficiently relented – George of Clarence and his wife Isabel. The Countess Anne and Anne, her other daughter, could not have left their sanctuary at Beaulieu and it would have been a difficult journey for Montagu's widow Isabel and her children if they still resided in the north. The Stanley, Fitzhugh and Hastings families may have felt that a public display of grief was inappropriate in the circumstances, and the same may have been true of the brothers' only surviving uncle, Edward, Lord Bergavenny, who had fought against them at both Barnet and Tewkesbury, and their now ageing aunts. Memorials may have been erected over their graves after a decent interval, but they were destroyed, together with the other family sepulchres, at, or shortly after, the Dissolution. The tangible reminders perished: only the legend survived.

II

All Warwick's present and former brothers-in-law became embroiled in these conflicts (all, that is, with the exception of the 'retired' Arundel), and all experienced changes of fortune as decisive as those of the two kings. The Earl of Oxford joined Warwick in arms in the summer of 1469 before the ink on his pardon was scarcely dry, and Edward's flight at the beginning of October 1470 allowed him to settle scores with his old enemy Worcester.

Worcester had added to his reputation for harshness by having twenty of Warwick's men who had been captured at sea impaled at Southampton in July, and was apprehended, disguised as a shepherd, in the forest of Weybridge (Huntingdonshire), after a servant who was helping him had tried to buy food with an unusually valuable coin. He was tried before Oxford, who had succeeded him as constable, and sentenced to be executed on 17 October, but so many people pressed to catch a glimpse of him that he was unable to reach the scaffold until the following day. His final request to the executioner, to strike off his head with three blows in honour of the Trinity, typified his uncompromising and enigmatic attitude to life generally. He was, says Kendall, 'more likely to weep at a torn manuscript than a severed head'.[4]

The Earl of Oxford joined Warwick and Clarence in France after the failure of the Lincolnshire rebellion, and was with them at Angers when Warwick was reconciled to Queen Margaret. He returned with them to England in September 1470, lodged himself in the London house of his brother-in-law, Lord Hastings, and bore the sword of state when King Henry was re-crowned in St Paul's. His men prevented Edward IV from landing near Cromer in Norfolk in March 1471 (forcing the King to make for the Humber), but were routed by Edward at Leicester on his march southwards on 3 April. This defeat, and Clarence's defection, would have turned many men's thoughts towards compromise, but Oxford was 'desposed in extrem malice agaynst the Kynge',[5] according to the Yorkist writer, and advised Warwick to remain firm. He commanded the right wing of the Lancastrian army at Barnet where his initial success had disastrous consequences. His men scattered the forces of Lord Hastings who opposed them, but on returning from the pursuit they were mistaken for Yorkists (Oxford's badge of a mullet, or star with streams of light, was confused with King Edward's 'sun in splendour') and fired on by their own men. The tide of battle turned in Edward's favour, and Oxford fled to Scotland as Warwick and Montagu fell.

A letter that Oxford wrote to Margaret, his wife, either just after his men were defeated at Leicester or shortly after Barnet, survives in the Paston collection, and shows he never doubted her loyalty even when things were not going well:

Right reverend and worshipful lady, I recommend me to you, letting you weet [know] that I am in great heaviness at the making of this letter; but thanked be God I am escaped myself, and suddenly departed from my men; for I understand my chaplain would have detrayed [betrayed] me: and if he come into the country let him be made sure [i.e. apprehended] &c.

Also ye shall give credence to the bringer of this letter, and I beseech you to reward him to his costs; for I was not in power at the making of this letter to give him, but as I was put in trust by favour of strange people &c.

Also ye shall send me in all haste all the ready money that ye can make; and as many of my men as can come well horsed, and that they come in divers parcels [small groups].

Also that my horse be sent, with my steel saddles, and bid the yeoman of the horse cover them with leather.

Also ye shall send to my mother, and let her weet [know] of this letter and pray her of her blessing, and bid her send me my casket by this token; that she hath the key thereof, but it is broken.

Also ye shall send to the Prior of Thetford, and bid him send me the sum of gold that he said that I should have. Also say to him by this token; that I showed him the first privy seal, &c.

Also let Paston, Felbrig, and Brews, come to me.

Also ye shall deliver the bringer of this letter an horse, saddle, and bridle.

Also ye shall be of good cheer, and take no thought [do not be concerned], for I shall bring my purpose about now, by the grace of God, whom have you in keeping.'[6]

Oxford was clearly one of life's optimists, but Margaret may have been only partly reassured.

III

The other three active brothers-in-law played very different roles in these troubles, Lord Hastings committing himself to Edward IV and sharing his exile, Lord Fitzhugh supporting Warwick, his long-term ally, and

Lord Stanley being all things to all men after his usual fashion. William Hastings was the eldest son of a knightly family whose principal estates lay in Yorkshire and Leicestershire. His father, Sir Leonard, had been a member of Richard, Duke of York's council, and this connection allowed him to meet, and become close to, York's son Edward. He served as sheriff of Warwickshire and Leicestershire during the Duke's second protectorate in 1455–56, and was fortunate to be pardoned after the rout at Ludford; but his gratitude to King Henry ran no deeper than his master's, and he again risked everything by joining young Edward in the campaign that brought him to the throne. His reward was to be summoned to Parliament as Baron Hastings of Hastings in July 1461, and to be given the recently widowed Katherine Neville as his wife.

King Edward also appointed William to the intimate and influential office of chamberlain, and confirmed his new status by endowing him with estates in the East Midlands forfeited by the Lancastrian peers Roos and Beaumont. Warwick made him steward of all his lands in Leicestershire, Rutland and Northamptonshire, and he was granted the chamberlainship of North Wales after the Earl's first coup against Edward in 1469. Probably Warwick hoped to make him an ally against the King – he clearly regarded him as more than just another Court favourite – but Hastings's loyalty was unshakable. He was active in brokering Edward and Clarence's reconciliation during King Henry's brief 'readeption', and the goodwill he had nurtured in his Midlands heartland throughout the decade bore fruit when Edward returned to recover his kingdom. Only a limited number of supporters had joined the Yorkist army as it moved southwards, but:

> At Leycestar came to the Kynge ryght-a fayre felawshipe of folks, to the nombar of iij^m [3,000] men, well habyled for the wers, suche as were veryly to be trustyd, as thos that wowlde uttarly inparte with hym at beste and worste in his qwarell, withe all theyr force and myght to do hym theyr trew service. And, in substaunce, they were suche as were towards the Lorde Hastings, the Kyngs Chambarlayne, and, for that entent above sayd, came to hym, stiryd by his messages sent unto them, and by his servaunts, frinds and lovers, suche as were in the contrie.[7]

Hastings had a hard time at Barnet where, as we have seen, his forces were routed by those of his brother-in-law Oxford, but he successfully commanded the right wing of the Yorkist army at Tewkesbury three weeks later.

Hastings seems to have been well liked by nearly everyone who knew him. There is no reason to doubt Thomas More's later assessment that he was an 'honorable man, a good knight and a gentle ... a loving man and passing wel beloved, very faithful and trusty ynough, trusting to much', and even Richard, Duke of Gloucester, we are told, 'loved him wel, and loth was to have loste him', when he had him beheaded in 1483.[8] Only Queen Elizabeth and some members of her family are said to have born him ill-will, the Queen because 'shee thoughte hym secretelye familyer with the kynge in wanton coumpanye'[9] and her son Dorset because of the mistresses they had tried to entice from one another. It was perhaps inevitable that Hastings and some of the Woodvilles would be rivals for King Edward's affections: but whatever his failings, there can be no doubt that his friendship with, and his loyalty towards, his royal master transcended all else.

It is unusual to find direct references to the personality and character of a fifteenth-century personage, and the information available for the life and career of Henry, Lord Fitzhugh, is much sparser. Henry was a long-standing ally of the Neville family, supporting the Earl of Salisbury in his dispute with the Percies in the early 1450s and serving with him as a member of the first protectorate council. In spite of this he was with Queen Margaret before the battle of Wakefield – perhaps, as Professor Hicks suggests, he was 'unable to absent himself'[10] – but he did not fight for the Lancastrians at Towton and was soon received into Edward IV's favour. His record during the 1460s was one of service and loyalty to the new dynasty – he was appointed Warwick's lieutenant, or deputy, in the West March in 1466 – but his old allegiance to the Nevilles reasserted itself when the Kingmaker fell out with King Edward in 1469–70. He was involved in Robin of Redesdale's uprising (his son, Sir Henry, and Sir William Parr, his son-in-law, fought on the rebel side at Edgecote),[11] and he stirred an insurrection in the North country in July 1470 shortly before Warwick and Clarence returned to England. This was never a real threat to the Government because the rebels soon realised their position was hopeless and sought refuge in Scotland, but it succeeded in drawing Edward away from the south where the Lancastrian lords intended to land.[12] Curiously, the King then pardoned him, together with his wife Alice, their five surviving sons and their daughters, Elizabeth and Anne, Anne's youthful husband Francis Lovel and Lovel's sisters Joan and Frideswide (who were presumably members of the Fitzhugh household), only weeks before he was himself forced into exile. Henry was assured of the goodwill of Warwick and the Lancastrian peers if they triumphed, but had left the door open in case they failed.

Warwick did, of course, succeed – at least in the short term – but there is no evidence that Fitzhugh was again active on his behalf. He does not seem to have been present (on either side!) at either Barnet or Tewkesbury, and died on 8 June 1472. He may have been ill by 1471 and unable to play an active role in either war or politics, but this is not to say that he did not welcome the opportunity to simply await the outcome. The restored King Edward would presumably have regarded him with a measure of suspicion, but his death allowed his heir and family to make a fresh start.

The events of the period 1469–71 created difficulties for most Neville relatives and retainers who had previously given their loyalty to King Edward, but few negotiated the pitfalls as adroitly as Eleanor's husband, Thomas, Lord Stanley. Thomas had succeeded to the barony when his father died on 11 February 1459, and faced his first test six months later when Queen Margaret ordered him to intercept his father-in-law Salisbury before the battle of Blore Heath. His response was to stand largely aloof from the conflict (although it is alleged that he prevented some Cheshire levies from joining the Queen while secretly sending aid to Salisbury) and the day after the battle he wrote to Margaret proffering his excuses and to Salisbury congratulating him on his escape! The Parliament that met at Coventry in November petitioned for his attainder, but Margaret, who was aware of the great influence he wielded in Lancashire and Cheshire, preferred an unreliable friend to a committed enemy. The stage was set for the rest of his career.

Stanley was with Henry VI at Northampton, but became a member of the Yorkist Council soon after the battle and was party to the agreement that settled the Crown on Richard, Duke of York and his heirs. He did not, apparently, fight at either Wakefield or Towton, but 'proved' his loyalty to the new government by helping Warwick and his other brothers-in-law besiege the Lancastrian-held northern castles in the early 1460s. There can be little doubt that he was on good terms with Warwick – he resided at Middleham for thirteen days in 1465–66 for example – but any new-found loyalty or friendship did not diminish his instinct for self-preservation. He declined to assist the Earl and Clarence when they rode to Manchester after the failure of the Lincolnshire Rebellion in March 1470, but helped them restore King Henry when they returned in the autumn. It seemed that he would now stand or fall with Warwick and the Lancastrian party; but his younger brother, Sir William, was among the first to join Edward IV after the Yorkist exiles landed at Ravenspur, and he somehow managed to avoid committing himself to either Warwick or Edward before Barnet. A decisive move by Stanley would have seriously threatened Edward's chances of regaining his kingdom, and Edward rewarded his 'neutrality' by appointing him steward of his household late in 1471.

We have no direct information of how the Kingmaker's sisters fared during this period of trouble, anxiety, and ultimately sadness, but Warwick's death was the culmination of a process that had threatened all of them with ruin. Three of their husbands had been exiled at different times (Fitzhugh in Scotland, Hastings in Holland, and Oxford in France) and the fourth, Lord Stanley, would probably have joined them but for his skill in backing the right horse at the right moment. It was some consolation that Hastings had recovered his former position while Fitzhugh and Stanley had been pardoned their indiscretions; but the family had lost not only its two most senior members but also much of its authority and reputation. Did Eleanor, Alice, Katherine and Margaret blame Warwick for creating the situation that had caused them so much trouble, or did they still secretly admire him; and did they commiserate with and try to help one another when some were in the ascendant and others in difficulty? No comment or correspondence survives unfortunately, but it would be hard not to admire a brother who bestrode national politics as Warwick did (even if he ultimately overreached himself), and uncharitable not to help a sister whose husband found himself on the wrong side of the argument. In the end only Margaret emerged from the dilemma with longer-term problems, but all the sisters would have been aware that their political capital had been devalued. A traitor's siblings would find it less easy to obtain favours – or even influential new husbands if they had need of them – than if they still had a powerful brother at court.

6

THE SISTERS IN THE SECOND REIGN OF EDWARD IV

The 1470s did indeed prove to be a time of considerable difficulty for many of the surviving members of the Neville family. Archbishop George died in 1476 after spending several years in prison – he had been in treasonable contact with the exiled Earl of Oxford – and young George, his namesake and nephew, faded into obscurity. He was degraded from his dukedom of Bedford in 1478 and the direct male line of Richard, Earl of Salisbury and Alice Montacute ended when he died five years later. Salisbury's next brother, George, Lord Latimer, passed away in December 1469 while the events described in the previous chapter were unfolding and Edward, Lord Bergavenny, the youngest, lived until 1476. They both left sons to succeed them, but none could fill the vacuum left by the Kingmaker. They remained junior members of the peerage at best.

Eleanor, the third sister, died soon after King Edward recovered his kingdom, presumably in London since she was laid to rest in St James's Church, Garlickhithe, in the city. There is no evidence that her remains were subsequently reinterred at Burscough Priory, the Stanley family mausoleum in Lancashire, although an effigy of her was incorporated into Lord Thomas's own monument after he was buried there in 1504. Thomas must have felt her loss keenly – she had borne him many sons and assiduously minded his interests – but may not have been sorry that his connection to the now discredited Nevilles had been severed. He married Margaret Beaufort, heir-general of the House of Lancaster, in 1472 and came to exercise greater power and influence, both at Court and in the north-west of England, than he had in the previous decade. We will never know if the thought that, one day, he might find himself the husband of the Queen of England ever occurred to him, but the possibility cannot be entirely ruled out.

Margaret Neville's husband, the Earl of Oxford, had unequivocally supported the Lancastrian restoration, and she was to suffer the consequences for the next fourteen years. She was living in St Martin's sanctuary in April 1472 – a concerned Sir John Paston remarked that 'I heer no word of hyr'[1] – and was still in difficulties five years later when Paston noted that 'the goode lady hathe nede of helpe and cowncell howe that she shall doo'.[2] She had no right to jointure since her husband was still living, and according to Fabyan, was obliged to live on charity or what she might get by her needle.[3] Her kinsman, John, Lord Howard, gave her 20s in August 1481 and the same amount a year later, donations we could probably trace to the 1470s if his accounts had survived for this period.[4] She was formally pardoned by King Edward in 1475 and again in 1479, but it was not until 1481 that she was granted £100 per annum 'on account of her poverty',[5] the money coming from customs and subsidies yielded by the ports of London, Sandwich, and King's Lynn. This was continued by Richard III (with Poole in Dorset taking the place of Lynn), but Richard had, after all, been given her husband's estates after Barnet. She seemed destined to spend the rest of her life as a virtual outcast, and her surviving siblings may have helped her as unobtrusively as they could.

All the sisters' lives had been temporarily disrupted by the conflicts of 1469–71, but none of their troubles were as permanent or long-lasting as those experienced by their sister-in-law, Warwick's widow Anne Beauchamp. Anne had returned to England at the same time as Queen Margaret and found sanctuary in Beaulieu Abbey (Hampshire) after she heard of the death of her husband at Barnet. She doubtless hoped that George of Clarence, her son-in-law, would help make her peace with King Edward, but found that he was more interested in securing the bulk of the Warwick lands for his wife, Isabel. Isabel was her late father's eldest child, but legally, was only one of several potential beneficiaries. Many of Earl Richard's northern and western Neville manors had been entailed on his nephew, George, Duke of Bedford, his nearest male relative; the Countess Anne would expect to receive a dower third of the income for her lifetime; and Isabel's younger sister, Anne, was entitled to half of the residue. The real prize was the Countess's vast Beauchamp-Despenser inheritance, but this, or more precisely Isabel's moiety of it, would be denied to Clarence until his mother-in-law died.

Anne Neville had been married to Prince Edward of Lancaster as part of the agreement by which her father had been reconciled with Queen Margaret, and was now a vulnerable young widow with few prospects. Her claims to her father's, and, ultimately, her mother's, lands could be safely disregarded; but the situation changed dramatically when Richard of Gloucester, the King's youngest brother, announced that he intended to marry her and would defend her interests against Isabel and Clarence. Clarence declared angrily that 'he [Gloucester] may well have my Ladye hys suster in lawe, butt they schall parte no lyvelod [property],[6] and tried to conceal her from his brother (disguised as a cookmaid, according to the Croyland chronicler),[7] until Gloucester found her and took her to the sanctuary of St Martin-le-Grand. Gloucester may have loved Anne, but was as ready to seize an opportunity as most other members of his class.

The two brothers duly pressed their suits in person before King Edward sitting in judgement in the Council chamber, the Croyland writer noting that 'so many arguments were, with the greatest acuteness, put forward on either side ... that all present, and the lawyers even, were quite surprised that these princes should find arguments in such abundance by means of which to support their respective causes'.[8] It was a situation that would have taxed even Solomon's wisdom and the best solution that Edward could come up with was to give most of the northern Neville lands to Gloucester and the bulk of the Beauchamp-Despenser estates (that still belonged to the Countess Anne) to Clarence. He doubtless hoped that this would satisfy them, but Clarence proved reluctant to accept a compromise that left him poorer than if he had been allowed to claim the whole inheritance through Isabel. Sir John Paston reported in November 1473 that 'ffor the most part that be abowt the Kyng have sende hyddr ffor ther harneys, and it [is] seyd ffor serteyn, that the Duke off Clarance makyth hym bygge in that he kan, schewyng as he wolde but dele with the Duke of Glowcester; but the Kyng ententyth, in eschyewying all inconvenyents, to be as bygge as they bothe, and to be a styffeler atweyn them; ... so what shall falle, can I nott seye.'[9] We do not know how Edward finally persuaded his brothers to preserve family unity, but in May 1474 an Act of Parliament formally deprived the Countess of Warwick of her properties and conferred them on her daughters and their husbands as though she was already dead. A second act barred the claims of young George Neville the following February, and completed one of the most cynical manipulations of an inheritance of this, or any other, time.

The Countess Anne appealed to the King, Clarence and Gloucester, to other members of the royal family, and petitioned Parliament prior to the passing of the legislation against her, but her protests fell on deaf ears. In June 1473 she was taken from Beaulieu to Middleham by one of Gloucester's retainers, Sir James Tyrell (a move that may have been designed to put pressure on Clarence to accept the King's judgment), and there she remained until her younger son-in-law was killed on Bosworth Field in 1485. Henry VII then obliged her to grant him all her properties with the single exception of the manor of Erdington (Warwickshire) where she presumably lived until her death in 1493.[10] John Rous described her as 'a full devout lady ... in hyr tribulacons sho [she] was ever to the gret pleasure of God full pacient to the grete meryte [merit] of her own sowl and ensample of all odre [other] that were vexid with eny adversyte'.[11] She had, remarkably, survived both her daughters and their acquisitive husbands, and all the other parties to the double wedding of 1436.

Alice and Katherine also had their difficulties in the 1470s, not as a consequence of the Readeption but because Henry, Lord Fitzhugh died in 1472 and William, Lord Hastings was frequently absent from home. Richard, Alice's eldest surviving son, was still only fourteen, and there was every likelihood that custody of his estates, together with his marriage and wardship, would be given to one of the King's trusted supporters. Alice was determined to keep everything in the family however, and had clearly both overcome her recent disgrace and convinced King Edward that she was the best person to look after her son's interests when she was appointed his guardian on 1 June 1475.[12] She also maintained an interest in the affairs of her son-in-law, Warwick's former ward Francis Lovel. The Duke and Duchess of Suffolk had been asked to manage Lovel's interests after the Kingmaker's death, but Alice probably continued to care for Joan and Frideswide, his two younger sisters. Anne, Lovel's young bride, would have joined him in the Suffolks' household, but it is likely that they both still thought of Ravensworth as 'home' and returned there whenever possible. It was in 1477, the year in which Francis attained his majority, that a dispute arose over the rightful ownership of some lands that his grandfather, William, Lord Lovel, had bought from the King's father, Richard, Duke of York, many years earlier. Lovel and King Edward agreed to allow two senior judges, Thomas Byllyng and Thomas Bryan, to act as arbitrators, but Francis also had to find three sureties who would guarantee he would abide by their decision. He turned to two Yorkshire gentlemen, James Charleton of Rykall and Ralph Wyclyff of Wyclyff, and to his mother-in-law, Lady Alice, who would (presumably) have had to find the lion's share of the £200 they agreed to pay if he defaulted.[13] Perhaps he was already acquiring the reputation for determination and rumbustiousness that would manifest itself in later years.[14]

William Hastings resumed his position as the King's chamberlain, a role that allowed him to regulate access to the sovereign but necessitated his presence in London or wherever Edward might be. He was also charged to add the West and North Midland regions formerly dominated by Warwick to his area of influence, and achieved this mainly by signing indentures (contracts of service) with many of the local gentry. He could not offer them lands to become his men and seldom money, but secured their goodwill by promising to assist them in 'all their rightful causes so far as law, equity and conscience required'.[15] Some choices would have been obvious, others more problematic – existing connections and local rivalries would often have determined who would, or would not, be invited to join his retinue – but the whole process would have required much patient negotiation as well as time spent cementing new relationships thereafter. There can be little doubt that he succeeded in establishing a substantial 'presence' in the area, just as he had in the East Midlands in the previous decade.[16] Perhaps the only losers were Katherine and their children who can have enjoyed little of his attention in what were otherwise quiet and peaceful years.

Katherine may have been left to manage the family household and estates largely unaided, but she could still rely on her husband to protect her interests in the wider world. In 1474 the King and Queen persuaded Hastings to allow Cecily, Katherine's daughter by Lord Harrington, to marry the Marquess of Dorset, Elizabeth's eldest son by her own first marriage; but Lord William was careful to ensure that his wife's Harrington jointure – 600 marks a year secured on various properties – would not be affected. Elizabeth was awarded the issues and profits of Cecily's lands for two years after she reached the age of fourteen, and Cecily was also empowered to grant them to her husband; but Katherine was to retain her portion of the Bonville-Harrington inheritance 'during her life'.[17] We cannot say that her rights would have been disregarded in other circumstances, but her husband's position and influence meant that she could rest easy on this score.

II

King Edward would have wanted to settle his brothers' differences and restore harmony under any circumstances, but his decision to renew the Hundred Years' War with France gave the matter added urgency. The royal family and aristocracy would be more likely to succeed in any enterprise if they were united, but did Edward really think he could better the dismal record of Henry VI's Government? His reasons for undertaking the enterprise (as given by the Chancellor in a speech to Parliament), were that an attack on France would preempt King Louis's unfriendly intentions towards England and make the Channel safer for English shipping; that foreign war would act as a safety valve (he acknowledged that, since the Conquest, internal peace had never prevailed for long 'in any king's day but such as have made war outwards'); and lastly, that it would provide lands and livelihoods for younger sons. His arguments were based almost entirely upon considerations of internal security and prosperity, and it is in stark contrast with Henry V's propaganda that he failed even to mention the English claim to France until he reached the fifth of his eleven pages and then disposed of it in a mere fourteen lines! Edward had, it may be inferred, recognised the futility of his predecessors' greater ambitions, but still thought that he and his country would benefit from putting pressure on Louis XI.

An alliance with the Dukes of Burgundy and Brittany, the last two semi-independent French princes, formed the cornerstone of his policy, but both were probably greater enemies of the King of France than they were friends of England. They would miss no opportunity to make life difficult for King Louis and dissuade him from encroaching on their territories; but they were, in the last resort, Frenchmen, and replacing him with an Englishman was an entirely different matter. The English Parliament granted money in quantities unseen for a generation, but King Edward still had recourse to 'benevolences', personal gifts from wealthy subjects extracted by charm or fear according to circumstances. The campaign would not be hindered by a lack of resources regardless of how much it might achieve.

The army that Edward assembled for this enterprise has been described as one of the largest ever to leave English soil, although few of its members had direct experience of Continental warfare. The Earls of Arundel and Oxford were inevitably absent, but the other two present and former Neville brothers-in-law both contributed substantial contingents. Lords Hastings and Stanley each brought forty men-at-arms and 300 archers for which Hastings received £966 18s 6d and Stanley £966 17s 6d per quarter including their own remuneration of 4s a day.[18] They embarked for France on 4 July 1475, but their hopes of success were dealt an early blow when Duke Charles appeared with only a small bodyguard instead of the strong force he had promised. His refusal to let the English into any of the towns he controlled only exacerbated their sense of isolation, and when he left to rejoin his main army Edward lost no time in entering into negotiations with King Louis. The outcome was that the two monarchs met on the bridge at Picquiqny on 29 August where Louis effectively bought Edward off with the promise of £15,000 within fifteen days, a large annual pension, a marriage between the dauphin and Princess Elizabeth for which he would provide a £60,000 jointure, and improved trade between their two countries. Edward was no Henry V and his 'victory' was no Agincourt; but it undoubtedly benefited his country more than if he had engaged in a long and ultimately disastrous war.

William Hastings was one of a number of senior noblemen effectively bribed not to oppose the agreement, although he pointedly refused to give Louis's representative a receipt. Philip de Commines records how the King granted him a pension of 2,000 crowns (£400) a year (notwithstanding that he was already receiving 1,000 from the Duke of Burgundy), and sent one Pierre Clairet to England with the first instalment. The cunning Louis wanted written proof that some of King Edward's senior counsellors were taking his money, but Hastings had no intention of obliging him even when Clairet slyly suggested it was only to prove that he (Clairet) had not embezzled it. '"Master Clairet",' Commines has Hastings say, ' "what you desire is not unreasonable, but this present proceeds from your master's generosity, not from any request of mine; if you have a mind I should receive it, you may put it into my sleeve, but neither letter nor quittance will you have from me; for it shall never be said of me, that the High Chamberlain of England was pensioner to the King of France, nor shall my receipt be ever produced in his chamber of accounts." ' Clairet, we are told, 'urged the matter no farther, but left the money, and returned his answer to the King, who was highly displeased at his not bringing a receipt; but he commended and valued the lord chamberlain above all the King of England's ministers, ever after paid him his pension constantly, and never asked for his receipt.'[19]

King Louis may have hoped that when Edward returned home without glory or booty his over-taxed subjects would overthrow him, and was disappointed that a popular uprising did not relieve him of the obligation to pay the promised annuities. Edward, on the contrary, seems to have enjoyed the support of most Englishmen, and attempts to challenge his authority within the country during this period were no more successful. His main protagonist was George of Clarence who, as we have seen, was disappointed that the Warwick inheritance settlement had not given him everything, and who had always treated his brother's forgiveness lightly. As early as 1472 he was suspected of conspiring with his wife's surviving uncle, Archbishop Neville, and the exiled Earl of Oxford, and when, next year, Oxford landed in Essex, he was said by the Milanese ambassador to have sent the King of France a list of those who had promised to support him, which included twenty-four lords, knights and gentlemen and *one duke* (my italics). Nothing could be proved however, and matters only came to a head when the Duchess of Clarence died shortly after bearing her fourth child on 22 December 1476. Charles of Burgundy was slain at Nancy two weeks later, and his widow, Margaret, proposed that her brother Clarence marry the heiress, her step-daughter Mary. This would have made Clarence one of the richest men in Christendom and allowed him to pursue Duke Charles's ambition to become King of Burgundy: but the plan was vetoed by King Edward on the grounds that he would then be obliged to support his brother against France. Edward had no intention of jeopardising his French pension, and lamely offered the Burgundians Earl Rivers, his brother-in-law, instead.

The result was that Clarence withdrew from Court in high dudgeon, behaved lawlessly in his own territories, cast aspersions on Edward's legitimacy, and declared openly that the Crown had unjustly executed one of his followers who had been charged with treason. The King initially disregarded these thinly veiled challenges to his authority, but finally lost patience and sent his brother to the Tower in June 1477. He was brought to trial the following January when, to everyone's surprise, the charges included not only his recent misdemeanours but also the novel accusation that he had secretly kept an exemplification of an agreement made in 1470 that recognised him as heir to the throne if Henry VI's issue failed in the male line. No evidence was produced to corroborate this extraordinary story, and commentators like the Croyland chronicler and Polydore Vergil were inclined to be both sceptical and bewildered. Clarence could have been charged with the lesser offences, deprived of some of his lands, or left in the Tower to cool his heels; but harbouring ambitions to the throne was treasonable and punishable by death. The implication is that another, secret, matter was fuelling the King's consternation, perhaps the story that Richard of Gloucester subsequently used to justify *his* usurpation, that Edward's marriage to the Queen was invalid and his children not entitled to succeed him. This allegation, if true, would have allowed Clarence to work a lot of mischief, and may be the real reason why he was executed (after being condemned by a pliant parliament in which Lord Hastings's retainers were prominent) on 18 February 1478.

The three surviving sisters would have heard of these events as word filtered to the provinces, but they would have made little difference to Margaret in her penury or to the widowed Alice. Katherine was perhaps relieved to learn that her husband had returned safely from France, and would have had further cause for satisfaction when he told her of King Louis's pension and how he intended to spend the money. Hastings had already embarked on major building works at his principal seat of Ashby de la Zouch in Leicestershire, a reconstruction that included the tower which bears his name and the nearby church dedicated to St Helen, and it is probably no coincidence that he also began to rebuild the castle at Kirby Muxloe, 17 miles away, in 1480. His plan was again to enclose an existing manor house within larger fortifications, but, wealth apart, why did he choose to construct fortifications at this time and on this scale? The most likely answer is that both buildings were designed as outward expressions of his authority, perhaps emulating Ralph, Lord Cromwell, Henry VI's treasurer, whose building works at Wingfield (Derbyshire) and Tattershall (Lincolnshire) seem to have provided the inspiration for the renovations at Ashby and Kirby.[20] Kirby was unfinished when Hastings met his untimely death in 1483, but few who passed by and saw the initials 'W H' and the family crest, the maunch, or sleeve, picked out in blue against a red background, could doubt that it belonged to a man who was a power both in the region and in the realm at large.

Hastings could not have indulged these projects without royal approval any more than he could have retained the services of large numbers of knights and gentry, but King Edward's approach to the problem of delegating authority was potentially, disastrously, flawed. Earlier rulers had preferred to share power in the localities between numbers of mutually jealous, watchful, lesser noblemen, but Edward chose to place large areas under the authority of a small coterie of trusted, very powerful, followers. His experience at the hands of Warwick (who had turned this might against him) ought to have alerted him to the dangers inherent in such a system; but the events of 1469–71 notwithstanding, he extended William Hastings's influence in the Midlands after he recovered his kingdom, and made Richard of Gloucester more powerful than Warwick in the North. Gloucester secured the allegiance of Alice Fitzhugh and her family (a process assisted by his marriage to her niece Anne and by his burgeoning friendship with her son-in-law Francis Lovel); but it was naive to pretend that this loyalty was unconditional or that it could never be turned against the reigning monarch. The Fitzhughs had put their personal fidelity to their regional 'good lord' before their obligation to the king in 1470, and Edward may not have appreciated that transferring their allegiance to Gloucester did not necessarily secure it for himself.

The last years of King Edward's reign were perhaps as settled and as peaceful a time as anyone had experienced that century, but great events were unfolding that would dramatically change the lives of two of the sisters and make at least some difference to the third. Edward was a large man with large appetites, as addicted to gluttony as he was to women, but few would have expected his constitution to fail him at the age of forty. His eldest son, Prince Edward, was still, at twelve, a few years short of being able govern for himself when his father died in April 1483, and this, crucially, allowed antipathies that had been held in check during the King's lifetime to flare into mutual suspicion and hostility. The calm would be followed by the storm.

7

THE SISTERS AT HOME

We have already noticed that married women – the vast majority of them – make fewer appearances in the sources than men because the law did not allow them to hold land or initiate legal proceedings independently of their husbands. It is often difficult to glimpse or reconstruct their 'public' lives, and harder still to see them at work in their manors and castles absorbed in their daily routine. The reason for this is quite simply that no one would have thought such everyday occurrences worth recording; yet dealing with what were essentially domestic matters must have occupied a far greater proportion of the sisters' time than was spent assisting their husbands with the business of local or national politics. We must therefore try to recover something of this part of their existence, even though direct evidence is lacking and we can speak only in general terms.

Where was 'home'? They would all surely have kept fond memories of Middleham where they had spent part of their childhoods before their marriages took them to new and sometimes distant households. Joan spent her adult life at Arundel Castle in Sussex, while Cecily lived at her first husband's castles of Warwick and Hanley (Worcestershire) before moving to Great Eversden in Cambridgeshire after she married John Tiptoft.

Eleanor and Alice lived at Lathom in Lancashire and Ravensworth in North Yorkshire, the principal seats of their husbands Lords Stanley and Fitzhugh, although Alice spent part of her widowhood at West Tanfield (Yorkshire) where her presence would not rival that of her daughter-in-law. Katherine's days were bound up with Ashby-de-la Zouch and, to a lesser extent, with Kirby Muxloe, both in Leicestershire, while Margaret would have savoured life as the lady of Castle Hedingham (Essex) when she was first married and again after 1485. Where she lodged during the years her husband was in prison or exile, and when she herself was not in sanctuary, is unfortunately not known.

The sisters – a duchess, two countesses and three baronesses – were not all of identical status, but their roles and responsibilities in the domestic arena would have been very similar. A greater mistress would have had a larger home (and probably more of them!), greater economic and estate responsibilities and a larger, more diverse, army of servants; but the differences were essentially differences of scale. Their situations could, and did, change from time to time. Margaret's was affected by her husband's attainder, while Alice and Katherine both experienced the dubious freedom of a long widowhood. They would all have had many decisions to make while their husbands were away on the King's business, or engaged in fighting for or against him in the Wars.

A noblewoman's prime responsibility was to ensure that her husband and children had everything they needed when they required it. She had to plan ahead, never allowing her concern with one matter to distract her from another and never losing sight of the overall picture. Any shortfall in the yield of the family's own demesne lands would have involved her in sanctioning purchases from local farmers, and she would also have bought other items, expensive imported goods, for example, that the estate could not produce itself. Foods were salted and preserved in times of plenty to tide the family over the leaner months of winter, a process that meant that volumes, and the likely number of visitors, also had to be estimated well in advance. Wood would be gathered to heat spits and ovens, storage containers checked to make sure they were adequate, and coarse cloth bought to strain milk and cheese and for general cleaning purposes. Nothing could be overlooked or left to chance.

The same was true of clothes and the materials needed to make them, fine garments for herself and her family and liveries for her servants. A well-dressed lady wore a linen chemise, or undergarment, beneath long dresses made from brocades or silks. These would be complemented by fine woollen hose, shoes and a head covering (only young girls went bareheaded), and would be lined or trimmed with fur or velvet. A finely woven girdle, necklaces, or brooches, added further decoration, everything being carefully chosen to reflect the wearer's rank in society. The wardrobe provided for her husband and children would have been no less in keeping with their status and ages, while the servants' liveries probably formed part of their annual remuneration. Nightwear ranged from nothing to an undergarment and nightcap according to the degree of modesty required.

Running a household meant that the sisters had to deal with literally dozens of employees, businessmen and well-wishers, giving them advice and instructions and making a good bargain where necessary. In the thirteenth century most household staff had been men – ladies' maids and laundresses were often the only females engaged – because it was feared that relationships formed between servants would lead to a corresponding reduction in devotion to the lord or lady. This attitude had softened by the sisters' time when husbands and wives were sometimes employed together instead of being required to live apart if one was in service; but men still occupied all the important offices and would have discussed the running of the establishment with their employers on an almost daily basis. In every house there would be a steward or general manager, a chamberlain, squires who formed part of their master or mistress's inner circle and accompanied them on journeys, chaplains and singers who conducted services, scribes who wrote letters and kept records, cooks and others who prepared and served meals, and a host of lesser mortals who ranged from grooms to cleaners to boys who ran errands. There was, as we have seen, a rigid hierarchy of precedence and protocol, but noblemen and women recognised that they had an obligation to look after their servants and often regarded them as part of their extended family. Many servants doubtless felt a similar sense of loyalty, particularly when they had lived and worked in a household for many years.

But if running a great house was one thing, managing estates when her husband was away from home was quite another. Regular meetings with bailiffs and other officials would have required her to make hard-headed commercial decisions that did not contravene local custom (something she would be expected to understand even if she came from another area), and while much of the routine would be delegated she still had to supervise and bear the ultimate responsibility. New lettings, problems with arrears and dilapidations, and the threat of lawsuits were just some of the concerns that would have obliged her to assess a situation and take a decision she thought would meet with her husband's approval, even if she lacked his maturity and experience. She might also have exercised authority in the manor court on occasion, ensuring that fines were collected and records made of the proceedings, and could enfeoff (convey into trust) or litigate in respect of the lands she had brought to the marriage with her spouse's sanction. Some ladies even engaged in trade if commerce appealed to them and again, if their husbands would permit it. Inevitably, some of the sisters would have chosen to be more 'hands on' in these matters than others, but they would all have been concerned with them to a greater or lesser extent.

Unfortunately the accounts, letters and other documents that would have allowed us to see the sisters at work in some of these capacities have long since perished. There are a few chance survivals from the late Middle Ages – the household book of Dame Alice de Bryene of Acton in Suffolk for the year September 1412 to September 1413 is a good example[1] – but many similar records would have been discarded when they were no longer of current interest. The National Archives has an account of the keepers of the lands of Cecily's first husband, Henry, Duke of Warwick; a receiver general's account for 1488–89 and also a household payments account for 1490–91 kept by servants of Margaret's husband, the Earl of Oxford, can be found in the Essex Record Office and in the rather misleadingly named *Household Books of John, Duke of Norfolk and Thomas Earl of Surrey,* temp. 1481–90; and the Huntington Library in California has a fragment of an arrears roll for the lands of Katherine, Lady Hastings for the year 1501.[2] The implications of this last document will be discussed in Chapter Nine, but the others tell us only that Margaret had her own household administration (her husband's receiver general paid her £43 9s 10d in the year in question) and that she was fond of pears in season! A young man was paid 4d 'for bryngyng of payres to my Lady' on 25 September 1489, and the same sum was spent

on another 400 only three days later. She may also have been responsible
for the intense cleaning of Castle Hedingham that went on in the period
covered by the account. A William Rener was hired to clear rubbish 'and
other stuff' from the castle ditch 'a fore the chambur wyndo' and from the
court on 7 September 1490, and was paid 4s 8d 'for the caryage of rubysh
out of the castell and other fylth ... and for bryngyng of daube and cley [a
colourant] in to the said castell ... [and] for vij days laboryng', probably in
anticipation of Christmas, on 20 December. We cannot tell if all the sisters
had their own household budgets (although it is very likely that they did so),
but they would all have been concerned with matters such as these.[3]

The sisters' personal wealth must remain conjectural, but some indication
of Katherine's can be gleaned from her will (see Chapter Ten) and a number
of valuable items that Margaret owned jointly with her husband are noticed
in Earl John's last testament and/or his inventory. Among the items that the
Oxfords had acquired during their marriage and which still bore both their
arms were a bed of crimson satin or damask, a little flat cup of gold, covered
and decorated with suns, valued at £21 13s 4d, a goblet of gold with a cover
(£19 3s 4d), a ornate silver gilt spice plate and cover (£25 13s 4d), a pair of
silver gilt basins decorated with roses (£26 13s), two similar newer ones
adorned with suns worth £21 5s 4d, and 'v tapette [hangings] of tapestry
damaske werke'. The last four items are said to have borne 'my olde Ladies
arms', a phrase that might imply that they had once belonged to the Earl
and his mother, Elizabeth; but the corresponding entry in his will makes it
clear that Margaret 'my late wife' is meant.[4]

One of the principal functions of a great house – and of the lady who
supervised it – was to offer hospitality to a wide range of visitors. These
would have included senior tenants and tradesmen, itinerant friars who
brought welcome gossip from the wider world, members of Parliament
actively 'selling' the Government's policies, and, more importantly, local
gentry and others who desired 'lordship' and were prepared to pledge their
loyalty in return. Much fruitful discussion must have taken place on these
occasions – the 'business lunch' is hardly a modern invention – and an
assured, charming hostess who had all the arrangements at her fingertips
was a great asset. The fare offered had to be the best available – a lord had
to display his wealth and potential influence if he wished to impress his

visitors – and everything from the quality of the dinner service to the musicians who provided entertainment was geared to creating a favourable impression. Lavish generosity – what MacFarlane called 'conspicuous waste' – was acceptable, but meanness and thrift were not.

Hospitality was also extended to poor people who were undertaking journeys or had fallen on hard times, again for very similar reasons. A noble who could afford to feed a large number of impoverished men and women without counting the cost was again making a personal statement, and at the same time storing up merit for himself in heaven. When King Edward reburied his father, Richard, Duke of York, in the family mausoleum at Fotheringhay (Northamptonshire) in July 1476, more than 1,500 mourners were fed in large dining-tents, and as many as 5,000 persons who came to seek alms were given a penny. The *Great Chronicle* describes how Warwick 'was evyr hadd in grete favour of the comonys of thys land, by reson of the excedyng howsold which he dayly kepid in alle cuntrees where evyr he sojournyd or laye, and when he cam to London he held such an howse that vi oxyn were etyn at a brekeffast, and every tavern was full of his mete, for whoo[ever] that had any acqueyntaunce in that hows, he shuld have hadd as much sodyn & rost [boiled and roast meat] as he mygth cary upon a long daggar'. Lady Alice de Bryene gave money and quantities of grain and dried peas to poor people who resided on her estates at the turn of the fifteenth century, her farm workers received a penny at Christmas and Easter, and local houses of religious were supplied with wheat or barley on an annual basis.[5] The sisters were no doubt as generous as their circumstances permitted (although perhaps, as we will see, not always from the highest of motives) and may have felt that they were actively doing 'good'.

Diet in the fifteenth century was generally monotonous, being at the mercy of the changing seasons, the fluctuations of good and bad harvests, and the difficulties inherent in transporting and storing a commodity that was always perishable to a greater or lesser extent. Poor people ate mainly bread, vegetables and a little bacon, foods often frowned upon by the aristocracy whose eating habits reflected their wealth and social precedence. Their meals were distinguished by their emphasis on meat and fish – smoked, salted and dried seafish together with freshwater varieties taken from their own

1. Richard Neville, Earl of Warwick (the Kingmaker) and his wife Anne Beauchamp, from the family tree in the 'Beauchamp Pageant' (British Library). Redrawn by Geoffrey Wheeler.

2. Middleham Castle.

3. (*Above*) Effigies of William Fitzalan, Earl of Arundel and his wife Joan Neville, Fitzalan chapel, Arundel Castle, Sussex.

4. *(Inset)* Detail of the head of Joan Neville, Countess of Arundel, photographed during the restoration of the effigies and tomb.

5. Henry Beauchamp, Duke of Warwick.

6. Cecily Neville.

7. John Tiptoft (d. 1470), Earl of Worcester and his wives, Ely Cathedral.

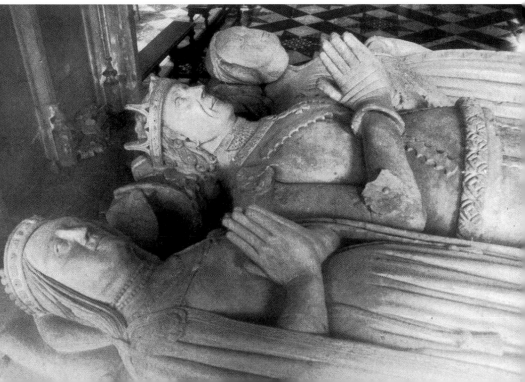

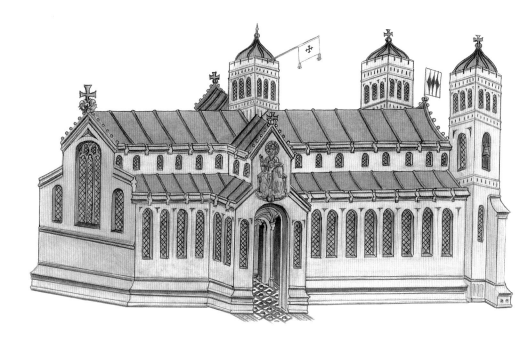

8. Drawing of Bisham Priory Church, Berkshire, from the Salisbury Roll (c.1463) (Duke of Buccleugh and Queensbury). Redrawn by Geoffrey Wheeler.

9. Cawood Castle.

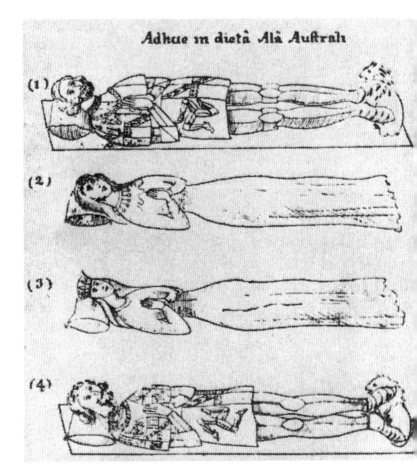

Adhuc in dictâ Alâ Australi

10. Stanley Effigies
in Ormskirk Church
(as drawn by Dugdale,
1664).

11. Ashby Castle.

12. Kirby Castle.

13. Ravensworth Castle.

14. Marmion Tower, West Tanfield.

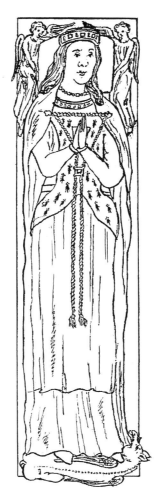
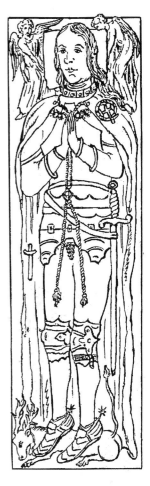

15. John de Vere, 13th Earl of Oxford and his wife Margaret Neville. Redrawn from Daniel King's original illustration of their funeral effigies at Colne Priory Church, destroyed *c*.1730.

16. The bridge at Castle Hedingham.

17. Warwick's signature.

18. Eleanor's signature.

19. Alice's signature.

20. Margaret's signature.

21. Katherine's signature (reproduced from the original in the Henry E. Huntington Library and Art Gallery).

22. Katherine's seal (reproduced from the original in the Henry E. Huntington Library and Art Gallery).

ponds – and by the expensive spices they used to colour food and disguise the sometimes dubious flavour! They preferred wine to ale – ale was the drink of the lower classes – and imported it mainly from Bordeaux (an English 'colony' until 1453), Burgundy, the Rhineland, Italy, Castile and the Levant. The 'butt of malmsey' in which the Duke of Clarence was allegedly executed was one of the sweet wines obtained from the near east, and would have been served to honoured guests with delicacies such as swans, herons and surprisingly, rabbits. Rabbits did not immediately adapt to the English climate when they were first introduced into this country in the thirteenth century, and warreners had to be employed to create artificial burrows and feed them in the winter. Every noble household had designated 'meat' and 'fish' days, Fridays being one of the latter but sometimes Wednesdays and Saturdays also. These were occasionally varied according to the feast and other partial fast days of the religious calendar, if, for example, Christmas Day fell on a Friday or if the diet was more limited on certain days in Lent. It was perhaps more than coincidence that most of Lady Alice de Bryene's visitors came to dine with her on 'meat' days!

We noted in Chapter One that medieval ladies did not nurture their children personally, but this does not mean that they did not care for them. Much time would have been spent discussing where and with whom they should live during their formative years, and most importantly, whom and when they should marry. It would have been every noble parent's ambition to place their son or daughter in a greater household in the hope that they would form friendships that would benefit the whole family, and plans were sometimes formulated before the children who were to fulfil them even existed. When William, Lord Hastings, agreed to help the widowed Elizabeth Woodville establish her right to some lands that had been settled on her and her late husband, part of the agreement was that her eldest son Thomas (the heir to the barony of Ferrers of Groby), would marry a daughter who might (or might not) be born to Hastings in the course of the next five or six years![6] The greatest danger was that a man might die before his heir was of age (the widow would lose control of the child's lands and marriage if the king gave the wardship to a powerful nobleman), or that a daughter's husband would succumb while she herself was still technically a minor. There were always predatory relatives ready to advance claims to estates that did not really belong to them, and parents and friends doubtless intervened on such occasions to secure a fair settlement for the distressed girl.

Widowhood clearly had its disadvantages, but it also gave a mature lady a degree of independence and control over her inheritance that she could never have enjoyed while her husband was living. A younger widow might still have to defer to her parents in the matter of her remarriage (usually, after being allowed a year to mourn her late spouse), but an older woman was free to determine her own status unless her late husband's will imposed particular restraints on her. Lord Fitzhugh's will has not survived, but William Hastings insisted that Katherine should retain her dower only 'so long as she continue unmarried', which may explain why she remained a widow for the rest of her life.[7] A new husband would have kept her of course, but there would have been nothing to stop her giving or bequeathing him valuables that her heir and other children expected to inherit. Whether rejection of remarriage also meant a rejection of sexuality is, of course, entirely unknown to us. Discreet liaisons would not have troubled the chroniclers, and the birth of a child out of wedlock would not have threatened the heir's position.[8] Any clues we might have gleaned from household records have been lost with the rest.

The sisters would have enjoyed little or no privacy as children, but probably found communal living less to their liking as they grew older. By the end of the fifteenth century it was customary for lords and ladies to take their meals in their private chamber rather than in the great hall in the presence of their households, and they increasingly, slept, washed, dressed and received visitors in their own rooms. This was not because they were more modest, or sophisticated, than their predecessors, but because they thought that separating themselves from others enhanced their status. They washed and bathed frequently, and covered their food, not because they were concerned about hygiene, but because such niceties were not available to ordinary people. Servants were required to have clean nails and to avoid coughing or spitting, not because anyone was worried about the spread of infection but because an obviously dirty or coarse servant would dishonour his mistress. In the same way exotic pets, caged birds and even bears were kept primarily as status symbols. They lacked the practical qualities of falcons, hunting dogs, and fine coach and warhorses, but were still measures, or yardsticks, of their owners' wealth.

The household day was structured around the principal religious services – Lady Mass and Compline were sometimes celebrated in addition to Matins, High Mass, and Evensong – and meant that those responsible for such matters had to calculate the passage of time. The sun was available to everyone (when it happened to be shining!) and marks could be made on a burning candle, but mechanical clocks that divided the day into 24 hours of equal duration became increasingly popular in the fourteenth century. Initially, these may have taken the form of bells controlled by mechanisms mounted in towers, but smaller, personal, versions were soon being installed in chambers. John, Duke of Bedford, Henry V's brother (d. 1435), had clocks in at least six of his household departments, including one that struck more frequently than the hour and noted some saints days on a ring, or wheel. The sisters doubtless grew up with similarly advanced mechanisms, and would have owned and used them daily when they had homes of their own.

The shortage of labour in the years after the 'Black Death' had resulted in many manors being let for rent rather than farmed directly, and noble households became more sedentary as the need to visit each estate in order to live off its produce diminished. But the sisters would still have travelled widely, particularly when there was a great family 'occasion', when they wished to discuss a child's marriage, or join a pilgrimage to Walsingham or another shrine. We do not know precisely *how* they undertook these journeys, but the practice of ladies riding side-saddle was becoming increasingly popular by the later fifteenth century and some noblewomen possessed 'carriages', decorated and upholstered covered carts. They would all have learned to ride astride in their youth, but may have come to prefer a gentler, slower mode of transport with the passage of time.

It is difficult in these days of high-speed travel to appreciate the comparatively slow pace of life at the end of the Middle Ages, and how long some journeys would have taken. H.S. Bennett's analysis of the *Paston Letters* has shown that the average distance covered by the various travellers was 34.8 miles per day,[9] although some managed as many as 51 or as few as 22. Male members of the family riding hard would have exceeded the 'norm' regularly, but their ladies, encumbered by household baggage, would have moved more slowly. Eleanor de Montfort accomplished some 26 miles a day in 1265 (on average), but Joan de Valence, Countess of Pembroke (d. 1316) could manage only 16.[10] When the Fitzhughs journeyed from Ravensworth to Bisham for Alice's parents' funeral it would have taken them approximately eight to ten days to reach their destination even if they made good progress and did not pause to rest *en route*. Many minor roads were 'broken, hollow and ruinous',[11] strewn with filth and garbage, and often little more than tracks made by men moving from village to village, bridge to bridge, or between fords. This was due partly to the lack of manpower that followed the plague years and partly to a shortage of money as the Hundred Years' War drew to its conclusion; but it also owed something to the decline of the monasteries (who had maintained some of them), and to the feebleness of a central government that allowed manorial and municipal authorities to avoid their obligations. Everyone who travelled risked being ambushed by thieves or enemies who hid in the abundant greenery, and the sisters would have been protected by well-armed escorts and by local guides employed to show them the safest passage. Regular, long-distance journeys had recognised halts where those who had spent the day on the road could, if necessary, change horses and obtain a bed for the night.

Travel was closely allied to communications since a letter or message could only travel as fast as the swiftest horseman. Wealthy ladies like the sisters could despatch personal messengers or servants, but more ordinary people had to rely on carriers (men who plied a particular route year in, year out and could be trusted) or upon anyone who happened to be going in the right direction. Such letters would seldom be delivered into the hands of the recipients, but would be left at inns, or the houses of third parties, from where the addressees could collect them. Some may have been discarded, or perhaps the travellers simply forgot on occasion; but the Paston correspondence suggests that very few failed to reach their destinations. Rude and barbarous the age may have been, but many people were perhaps more conscientious than they are today.

Latin remained the language of the Church and of legal documents, while Norman French may still have lingered in some polite aristocratic circles; but the sisters' surviving letters are all in English and there can be little doubt that they used English for everyday purposes. Most members of the aristocracy, together with the swelling business community, were literate by 1400, and English was becoming the language of society rather than merely a popular vernacular tongue. Henry V was the first ruler since Alfred to conduct royal business in English and to encourage its use by others (which is all the more remarkable when we consider that he meant to rule in France as well as England) and in 1422 the London Brewers Company resolved to keep their records in English because: 'Whereas our mother-tongue, to wit the English tongue, hath in modern days begun to be honourably enlarged and adorned, for that our most excellent lord King Henry V hath in his letters missive and divers affairs touching his own person, more willingly chosen to declare the secrets of his will, and for the better understanding of his people, hath with a diligent mind procured the common idiom (setting aside others) to be commended by the exercise of writing'. English became the chief medium for political verses – propaganda tracts written by clerks in, or on the fringes of, government service, and commissioned by the regime or by rich patrons opposed to it – and for public pronouncements made in bills posted on church doors and other public places. When Archbishop Scrope of York joined the 1405 rebellion against Henry IV he ordered that his grievances be 'written in English ... and set upon the gates of the city, and sent to curates of the towns for to be preached openly'.[12] The spoken word was still paramount – the Government was still obliged to communicate with the broad mass of its subjects through pronouncements made in the manor court and from the parish pulpit – but the written was beginning to make its mark.

We have no direct knowledge of how the sisters spent their leisure time. As children they probably enjoyed games such as skipping, leap-frog, marbles or blind man's buff, and when they grew to maturity their pastimes would have been those of their class. There were few noblemen and women who did not take pleasure in falconry and in hunting hares, harts, foxes, wolves and wild boars, although the latter two were becoming increasingly scarce. The bow was the weapon of the chase and remained a key element in English armies; but the fact that the Government found it necessary to compel every man to own a longbow and to practise shooting at the butts suggests that its popularity may have been waning by the middle of the century. It may already have been less popular than football, a game banned by at least three kings because it interfered with more martial pastimes but which was traditionally played on festivals such as Shrove Tuesday when violent melees involving large numbers of participants were commonplace. A primitive form of cricket was popular at all levels of society, and both the English and French royal houses favoured tennis, often played in an enclosed area such as a dried-up castle moat. Indoors, the most popular diversions were shovel-board (a game in which flat metal weights were pushed across a table marked with horizontal lines stopping as near to the opposite edge as possible), dice, cards, backgammon (all regularly prohibited to discourage gambling) and chess, which was so popular by the latter half of the century that Caxton made it the subject of one of his first printed books. All the sisters would have been expert needlewomen, and would have enjoyed reading, story-telling, listening to music, and entertainments provided by travelling players. Their amusements were simple by modern-day standards, but it is unlikely they were ever bored.

Success in all these activities would have been affected by the sisters' health or lack of it, and they would have been all too familiar with the illnesses that permeated medieval society and with their often highly inappropriate 'cures'. Medieval medicine was still largely governed by the theories of Hippocrates of Cos (b.c.460 BC) and Galen (b.c. AD 129) which taught that illness was caused by an lack of harmony between the four 'humours' of the body, choler or yellow bile (which was 'hot and dry'), phlegm or mucus ('cold and wet'), black bile ('cold and dry'), and blood ('hot and wet'). As patients they would have described any symptoms that were not self-evident (women were expected to remain covered at all times during consultations), and the physicians would have checked pulses and examined samples of urine and faeces to determine which humour, or humours, were responsible for the imbalance. These were then 'corrected' by purging and by dietary changes that took account of the heat, coldness, dryness, or moisture content of particular foodstuffs, all administered in accordance with the potentially favourable or unfavourable influences of the planets as determined by astrological tables. The most common therapy was bloodletting, the blood being extracted by the process of 'cupping' in which glass cups were applied to the patient's skin in such a way as to create a vacuum. Medieval people thought that blood circulated round the body only once a year and feared that, left to itself, it would stagnate and fail to move on to its next location. Bloodletting encouraged it to flow more freely and would, the doctors believed, produce benefits that outweighed the weakness resulting from its loss. Their lack of understanding clearly endangered the patient, and the risks increased dramatically if they decided to administer powerful substances such as mercury and arsenic after milder remedies made from spices, herbs or wild flowers had failed to produce an improvement.[13] The doses would be carefully calculated, but could readily give rise to suspicions that the patient had been poisoned, either by greedy children or an uncaring spouse.

It follows that people who became seriously ill often had little hope of recovery and the constant imminence of death made them morbidly (to our way of thinking) preoccupied with the afterlife even in their youth. The Church taught that the deceased would first enter purgatory – a kind of halfway house where their sins would be purged by suffering before they were (hopefully) allowed to reach heaven. No one knew how long a soul might spend in purgatory, and the belief that both the time and the ultimate destination could be influenced by the prayers of the living placed a considerable obligation on both testators and members of their families. It was for this reason that Katherine's husband William, Lord Hastings left money and valuables to thirteen churches and religious institutions to remember him in their prayers when he made his will in 1482, and John, Earl of Oxford asked that no fewer than 2,000 masses be sung or said for him after he died in 1513. Lord Henry and Lady Alice Fitzhugh founded 'a perpetual chantry of two chaplains to celebrate divine service daily in the chapel of St John the Apostle and Evangelist in the castle or manor of Ravenswath, co. York, for the good estate of the said Henry and Alesia [Alice] his wife and for their souls after death and the souls of the ancestors of Henry and the founder and benefactors of the house or hospital of St Giles by Brompton on Swale, co. York, to be called the chantry of St Giles in the said chapel; and to grant in mortmain to the said chaplains lands and rents not held in chief to the value of £10 yearly.'[14] A deceased relative's 'month mind' (the thirtieth day after his or her death) or obit (yearly anniversary) would be conscientiously and often elaborately commemorated. The living were conscious of their own shortcomings, and hoped that others would remember them in their turn.

The sisters' attitude towards death was an integral part of their approach to their Christian religion generally, and one of a number of obligations that their membership of the universal Catholic Church imposed upon them. Going to mass and making confession were serious obligations (not lifestyle choices as they often are nowadays), and they would have learned the three basic prayers of the Church (the Paternoster [Lord's Prayer], Apostles' Creed, and Ave Maria) and how to make the sign of the cross in childhood. It was Christianity rather than philanthropy that persuaded them to offer assistance to those who were less fortunate, and to devote large sums to repairing and rebuilding churches of which they were patrons.[15] A private household chapel was a status symbol that avoided rubbing shoulders with the peasantry in the local parish church; but conversely, it was in the monastic or parish church that they chose to be buried. It was here that the faithful, monks and people, would see their effigies and remember their souls in their prayers.

The later medieval nobility appear at first glance to have been exceedingly pious, and it is worth asking how much of this was attributable to genuine spirituality and how much to convention? Their almsgiving was often mechanical, and it is difficult to reconcile their avarice and tendency towards violence with a deeply-held commitment to Christian teaching. Cecily Neville, Warwick's aunt and Edward IV's mother, and Margaret Beaufort, Henry VII's mother, have gone down in history as two of the most pious ladies of their era; but the former continued to dabble in politics from the seclusion of her religious 'retirement', and the latter had accumulated vast wealth when she died in 1509.[16] The sisters were not the mothers –or wives – of kings, but there is no reason to suppose that their religion inhibited them from lining their own pockets (even if they gave some of it away subsequently) or doing what they could to improve their situation locally. We have no means of knowing how many of the seven corporal acts of mercy they each fulfilled personally. They may, and some or all probably did, feed the poor, give drink to the thirsty, house the stranger, clothe the naked, visit the sick, relieve the prisoner and bury the dead; but again, was it because this was what society, and particularly their peers, expected of them? The answer is perhaps that they were no more, or less, pious than most of their contemporaries, and that their main preoccupation was to have the best of this life while keeping a close eye on the next! It was not an easy balancing act, but they hoped that the good would compensate for the bad.

This then, was the sisters everyday 'routine' as far as we can now discern it. Comparisons with our own time are not very helpful – indeed it could be argued that no real modern parallels exist anyway – but their own lives were full of contrasts and apparent contradictions. They had large numbers of servants who relieved them of all routine duties: but servants had to be managed and the lady always bore the ultimate responsibility for the successful running of her household. They did not bring up their children on a day-to-day basis and often sent them to live with other people; but the success of their own family was central to their existence, and it was arguably a greater responsibility to undertake the oversight of another's child than if he or she had belonged to them. They were wholly subservient to their husbands and scarcely existed independently of them, but they fulfilled many 'male' duties in their spouses' often frequent absences and displayed considerable ability and self-confidence. It was not always an easy life, but the sisters undoubtedly accepted their lot and appreciated the privileges it brought them. Changing the hand fate had dealt them would not have entered their minds.

8

THE SISTERS IN THE REIGN
OF RICHARD III

*T*he Wars of the Roses might have ended with Tewkesbury and
Yorkist kings ruled England for centuries; but the political
consensus was again shattered after Edward died prematurely in
1483. Few doubted that Edward V, his eldest son, would succeed
him peacefully, but Richard, Duke of Gloucester, the late King's youngest
brother, stepped in and claimed that the throne was rightfully his. We will
probably never know if Edward IV had contracted an informal marriage
with Lady Eleanor Butler before he wed Queen Elizabeth – his promises
would have been made lightly and soon forgotten – but the powers-that-
be could have resolved the matter by crowning the boy-king if they had
wanted him to reign over them. Some noblemen, Lords Hastings and Stanley
among them, would have thought this a logical and acceptable solution, but
they were about to be overtaken by events.

Gloucester's first decisive act was to arrange a 'friendly' meeting with
young Edward and his Woodville entourage at Stony Stratford at which he
arrested Earl Rivers, the Queen's brother and several members of her family.
Hastings, Stanley and other councillors then in London had little love for

the overbearing Woodvilles and readily accepted Gloucester's explanation that they had been planning to deny him the protectorship during Edward's minority. It is impossible to know if Gloucester had a clear vision of the future or if his plans changed as events unfolded; but on 13 June 1483 he had Hastings, Stanley and others seized in the Council chamber, and Hastings summarily beheaded without trial. His 'excuse' was again that he had discovered a conspiracy against himself involving Woodvilles and others he had hitherto trusted; and although he had not, as yet, challenged Edward V's right to the kingdom, it is difficult to avoid the conclusion that he was effectively clearing his path to the throne.

Thomas Stanley was wounded in the fracas in the Council chamber and arrested; but he was not a potential leader of the opposition like Hastings and was allowed to resume his position at court. It was Hastings who, with his powerful Midlands-based retinue, had both the might *and* the will to frustrate Gloucester's ambitions, and his elimination was essential if Edward V was to be deposed and there was to be an orderly and peaceful succession. Gloucester, Hastings and Rivers had all shared Edward IV's exile in 1470–71, and had remained on good terms during the second period of Edwardian government. Rivers had agreed to submit a dispute about some lands in Norfolk to Gloucester's arbitration as recently as March 1483, and Hastings had sent him word of the King's death, urging him to come southwards as quickly as he could. The Croyland writer remarks that Lord William was heard to boast that the Woodvilles had been discomfited 'without any slaughter, or indeed causing as much blood to be shed as would be produced by a cut finger', [1] and both he and Rivers had clearly underestimated Gloucester's ability to act decisively. Duke Richard may have feared that he would have little security in an England ruled by Edward V and his mother's relatives; but his ruthlessness was remarkable even in that barbarous age.

II

Gloucester's coronation as Richard III was a magnificent affair, attended by the great majority of the nobility. This may, as some have suggested, imply that his accession enjoyed widespread approval; but the scattered opposition was now leaderless and it is more probable that many peers simply concealed their inner thoughts and bowed to the inevitable. Katherine Hastings was now officially the widow of a traitor, Margaret's husband, the Earl of Oxford, remained irreconcilable, and so the only sister invited to attend the ceremony was Alice Fitzhugh. She joined her daughter Anne, Viscountess Lovel (Francis Lovel had been made a viscount on 4 January), her daughter-in-law Elizabeth Burgh (her son Richard's wife), and nine other noblewomen who followed the Queen in three 'chares' (four-wheeled vehicles) decorated in crimson trimmed with gold and bearing the royal arms as the new monarchs processed to Westminster on the afternoon of 5 July. They wore long gowns 'made of vij yerdes of blue velvet and purfiled with v yerdes and a quarter of crymsyn satyn'[2] which the King had given them, the baronesses' being subtly differenced to distinguish them from the duchesses and countesses in the party. Riding behind on palfreys, and similarly dressed, were seven or more of the Queen's ladies-in-waiting including another of Alice's daughters, Elizabeth, the wife of Sir William Parr. The procession's slow and, it has been suggested, 'probably disorderly' progress was punctuated by stops at a number of places where Richard and Anne were regaled with singing and speeches arranged for them. These included the Standard, near Milk Street in Cheapside, and the Eleanor Cross in Wood Street, at one of which the Recorder of London presented them with purses of 1,000 and 500 marks to defray their costs. They were refreshed by wine and spices on arriving at Westminster Hall, and then retired to change their clothes before partaking of a substantial 'souper'.

Few involved in the proceedings can have slept much that night, and the four Fitzhugh ladies would have been attired in their coronation robes consisting of seven yards of crimson velvet purfled with four or more yards of white damask when the King and Queen entered Westminster Hall with their entourages at seven o'clock in the morning on 6 July. They all processed on ray cloth to the west door of the Abbey choir, the heralds being followed by the Abbot and Convent of Westminster, the Chapel Royal, the assembled abbots and bishops, eighteen newly made knights of the Bath, ten senior noblemen each bearing a symbol of royalty, and the crystal mace of the City of London carried by the Mayor. King Richard was accompanied by the

Bishops of St Asaph, Lincoln, Bath and Durham, and behind him walked the remaining earls and barons, three noblemen bearing the Queen's regalia, the Queen herself flanked by the Bishops of Norwich and Exeter, and a long train of ladies.

On reaching the Abbey, the royal couple were brought to their thrones which had been placed on a richly decorated stage between the choir and the altar, and the Archbishop formally presented the King to the people who acclaimed him as their sovereign. They were then led to the altar, flanked by their respective bishops, where the King made an offering before prostrating himself while the Archbishop prayed over him. He was then seated in a chair facing the Primate, heard a short sermon, and swore oaths that he would keep the laws of his predecessors, do justice, and defend the Church and its privileges. More prayers were then said as he again lay, or knelt, before the altar, while the Queen knelt and prayed at his side.

After a short pause the King removed some of his outer clothing, and was anointed with the holy oil of St Thomas on his hands, back, breast, shoulders (to symbolise strength), in the crook of his elbows (to symbolise wisdom) and on the crown of his head, in the form of a cross, symbolising glory. He was then vested with his royal garments and regalia, and the Archbishop crowned him seated in his chair by the altar. A ring was then placed on the fourth finger of his right hand, and he offered his sword at the altar and received it back again as a token that his strength and power should come from God. The sceptre was then placed in his left hand and the orb in his right, and he was blessed. The bishops approached and kissed him as he sat by the altar, and he was then led to his throne on the stage where he received the fealty and homage of his lords. The Bishops of Bath and Durham helped to support the Crown, while the Dukes of Buckingham and Norfolk assisted with the sceptre and orb.

The Queen was now brought to the altar by her supporting bishops, and after prostrating herself was partially disrobed and anointed with the ordinary oil of the catechumens on her breast and on her forehead in the form of a cross. A ring was placed on the fourth finger of her right hand, her crown on her head, and her sceptre and rod in her right and left hands. She was then led to her throne on the stage, curtseying as she approached the King, and it is probable that Alice Fitzhugh, her daughters and daughter-in-law were among the ladies who knelt beside and behind her while the Archbishop sang mass. The royal couple rose and returned to the altar twice during this service, making their offerings on the first occasion, and then confessing before receiving absolution and the sacrament on the second. The volume from which a bishop had read the Gospel was brought to them to kiss, followed by the Pax, a tablet bearing an image of the crucified Christ.

The mass being ended, the royal couple were taken to the altar before the shrine of St Edward (behind the high altar of the Abbey), where their crowns were laid and where they were re-dressed in their robes of estate. The smaller 'imperial crowns' were then placed on their heads, and, bearing their sceptres in their hands, they returned to their thrones on the stage. The procession then reformed and made its way back to Westminster Hall 'going in great triumph', where it dispersed, the King and Queen (and presumably most of the others), retiring to their chambers for a well-earned rest.

The great coronation banquet began shortly after four o'clock, the King sitting at the marble table of the King's Bench with the Queen on his left and the Bishop of Durham (deputising for the aged Archbishop of Canterbury) on his right. The guests were seated at four long tables stretching the length of the Hall, the Mayor, Aldermen and other leading citizens of London at the first on the left side, the Queen's ladies (including the Fitzhughs) at the second, the bishops, peers, judges and royal officers at the third, and the Barons of the Cinque Ports and others at the fourth. The two main courses were introduced by trumpets and brought in with great ceremony by the Marshal of the Hall, Sir Robert Percy, accompanied by other Household officials and the Duke of Norfolk, who was acting as Lord Steward, on horseback. The King was served on gold plate, the Queen on gilt and the Bishop of Durham on silver, and there was music and singing by the King's minstrels and the choir of the Chapel Royal who occupied a stage at the end of the Hall. During the second course, Sir Robert Dymock, the King's Champion, rode in on a silk-trapped charger and formally challenged anyone present who disputed his master's title to single combat. The response was a universal shout for 'King Richard', after which the Champion was given a cup of wine from which he drank and carried away as his fee. The kings of arms, heralds and pursuivants who occupied a stage to the King's right then descended, and Garter King of Arms, as the senior, proclaimed Richard King and Lord.

By now it was so late that the third course of the meal was dispensed with and torches were summoned, an indication of how long everything had taken. The lords rose and made their obeisance to the King and Queen, after which the royal couple departed to their chambers followed by their guests. There is no record of what happened during the next few days, but the King would certainly have heard mass the following morning, and there would have been more formal meals and perhaps dancing by the ladies in the evening. A tournament, with jousts, would have been held in keeping with tradition, and there can be little doubt that members of the extended Neville family used these opportunities to renew their acquaintance. Alice would have encountered her former brothers-in-law Lord Stanley and the Earl of Arundel (who could not excuse himself from this occasion) and her children, including her son Richard, now Lord Fitzhugh, would have become better acquainted with their cousins, Stanley's son Edward, Arundel's heir, Thomas, Lord Maltravers, the two George Nevilles (son and grandson of Edward, Lord Bergavenny), Richard Neville, Lord Latimer (George, Lord Latimer's grandson), and, of course, their new Queen, the Kingmaker's daughter Anne.[3] Recent events, Hastings's execution and Katherine's uncertain future would have been quietly discussed when circumstances permitted; but Richard III was now King of England, and even those who had reservations knew they had to come to terms with him. Some of the younger Nevilles may even have rejoiced at the elevation of one of their family, and thought that they had now, finally, overcome the stigma of Barnet; but Queen Anne was not long for this world and Richard's reign would be unexpectedly short.

III

It was inevitable that William Hastings's offices – and with them much of his influence – would pass into other hands after his execution since his son and heir, the sixteen-year-old Edward, was still legally a minor and inexperienced in politics and regional government. But the predatory ambitions of the new King and his supporters were not satisfied by the mere redistribution of patronage, and the vultures soon began to circle around the family's lands. There is no evidence that Lord William had actively plotted against Richard, and the King, his purpose accomplished, waived the customary Act of Attainder (thereby forestalling an inquiry into the alleged offences) and promised to be 'good and gracious soverain lord' to the widowed Katherine and her children 'not suffring theim to be wronged ne entreated contrary to oure lawes'.[4] But the royal munificence did not extend to the wealthy manor of Loughborough, the family's most valuable property, which, it was held, 'to us and oure derrest wif in hir righte belongethe' an assertion which, whatever its merits, had not, apparently, been made before.

The loss of Loughborough dealt a considerable blow to the family's position in northern Leicestershire, but worse was to follow. Francis Lovel was Katherine's sister's son-in-law, but this did not prevent him from claiming that their *caput honoris* of Ashby, the manor of Bagworth, and some properties which his attainted uncle Viscount Beaumont had held in the north-east of the county and in Lincolnshire were rightfully his. Lovel had no legal title to the lands in question – he had formally quitclaimed, or rescinded, his interest in Ashby (which his Zouch and Burnell ancestors had held of the Beaumonts) three years previously, Bagworth had been sold to the Hastings family by his father, Lord John Lovel[5] and William Beaumont (and his heirs and successors) had been deprived of their estates by Act of Parliament. But such niceties could not deter a man who was now among the greatest in the kingdom and who was prepared to use violence to achieve his objectives. In 1481, for example, he sent his retainer Sir Robert Markham and other followers to 'make an entre' into the Bishop of Winchester's manor of East Bridgford, near Nottingham, which he claimed as co-heir to the entailed lands of William Deincourt, his grandmother's brother;[6] and it is likely that trouble was again imminent when the King intervened to defuse the 'traverse and variaunce' which had arisen between Lovel and his cousin Henry, Lord Morley, for possession of the manor and lordship of Claydon, in Buckinghamshire, in December 1483.[7] He was, it must be said, doing no more than many of his kind would have done under similar circumstances and Katherine's vulnerability was only too plain.

The 'variaunce and grudge', as the deed calls it, was partially assuaged on 5 May 1485 when, after the 'mediation of frendes', Katherine agreed to give Lovel lands to the value of a third part of his uncle's properties to a maximum of 200 marks per annum (in addition to 200 marks in cash she had paid him already), in return for the peaceful enjoyment of Ashby and Bagworth and the residue of the Beaumont inheritance. Lovel promised to be 'good lord and cousin' to her and her son Edward, but was careful to emphasise that he had accepted the compromise because, in the words of the agreement 'the said variances cannot finally be appeased during the nonage [minority]of the said Edward Ld Hastings'.[8] It would appear that he intended to seek a more favourable settlement when Edward came of age in November 1487, and that his demands were part of a process designed to establish him as King Richard's viceroy in the Midland region. The Lovels had not resided at Titchmarsh, in Northamptonshire, the seat of their barony, for over a century; but Francis had enough local connections to begin the process of securing the loyalty of the gentry for the new government, and it was unlikely that the assurances that the King had previously given to Katherine would be allowed to inhibit him. The scheme ended with Richard's death at Bosworth, but it is hardly surprising that, two years later, the 'Yorkist' Edward Hastings fought for Henry Tudor – and against his arch-rival Francis Lovel – at the hard and crucial battle of Stoke.

We are not told who the 'frendes' who helped to negotiate the compromise between Katherine and Lovel were, but one person who could have sought to influence them was Katherine's sister and Lovel's mother-in-law, Alice Fitzhugh. Alice's concern for her daughter and her husband is writ large in the records of the next reign, and it may be significant that when Katherine made her will in November 1503 she left Alice 'oon of my standing cuppes [and] a bedd of tymbre'.[9] Alice undoubtedly helped her sister during the sometimes difficult years of her widowhood, and this, as we will see, was only one of a number of kindnesses which Katherine remembered with gratitude years later. The violent death of her husband and the assault on her family's properties must have transformed her hitherto secure, peaceful existence; but she had clearly put aside her grief to seek help where she believed she would find it and had done her best for Edward and her other children. Strength of character was a virtue the Neville ladies seldom lacked.

IV

Richard III survived a revolt led by Woodvilles and some of Edward IV's former household men in the late autumn of 1483 (the so-called 'Buckingham's Rebellion'), but was defeated and slain two years later by Henry Tudor, the last scion of the House of Lancaster. The alliance of old Lancastrians and disgruntled Yorkists that had been defeated at Barnet finally triumphed on Bosworth Field, but only after one of the most remarkable military upsets of the Middle Ages. King Richard could call on the resources of his kingdom and was a seasoned commander; Henry, on the other hand, lacked military experience, and had no way of knowing if his motley army of English, Welshmen and French mercenaries would gel in combat. It is still remarkable that Richard lost the battle, and interesting that the three men arguably most responsible for his defeat, the Earls of Oxford and Northumberland and Lord Stanley, all had Neville connections. The question is, of course, were these purely coincidental, or did the ghost of the Kingmaker have the final say?

John de Vere, Earl of Oxford had, as we have already noticed, been a constant thorn in the side of the Yorkist kings since long before 1471. After his flight to Scotland he went to France from where he master-minded attacks on Calais and attempted a landing at St Osyth in Essex. His efforts were at least partly financed by a successful campaign of piracy conducted from French and Scottish ports, and his depredations on the high seas continued until he captured St Michael's Mount in Cornwall on 30 September 1473. He was promised his life when the threat of desertion by most of his followers forced him to surrender the Mount four and a half months later, and spent the next ten years a prisoner in Hammes Castle in the Calais pale. Richard III ordered his transfer to England in October 1484, but he escaped to join Henry Tudor, taking his gaoler, James Blount, with him. He commanded Henry's vanguard at Bosworth where his military experience – particularly his decision to concentrate his men in wedge formation around the standards – contributed significantly to the Tudor victory. He had been in opposition for almost as long as his new master, and their long years of exile were ended by a single bold stroke.

Thomas, Lord Stanley, had married Henry's mother, Lady Margaret Beaufort, in 1472, but was too astute a politician to declare openly for his stepson's party. Both the Yorkist kings had forgiven his doubtful loyalty – Richard as recently as the fracas in the Council chamber which had culminated in Hastings's execution – and his steadfastness during 'Buckingham's rebellion' brought him lands and the senior position of Constable of England. Richard may not have trusted him entirely however – there had been difficulties over Hornby Castle and other lands which Stanley had disputed with the staunchly pro-Ricardian Harrington family – and when in the summer of 1485 he left the court to return to his family seat at Lathom (Lancashire), the King insisted that George, Lord Strange, his eldest son, remain behind. He pleaded illness when Richard summoned him to join the royal army before Bosworth, and when, shortly afterwards, it became apparent that his brother, Sir William, and other family members were in league with Henry, the King threatened to execute Strange if his father joined them. Stanley, in the event, retired as his stepson advanced, neither impeding nor joining him, and may not have been present on the battlefield. The Croyland writer and Vergil imply that he declined to join either army when ordered to do so, and Stanley himself said that he only met Henry for the first time two days after the victory.[10] It would not be surprising if he had kept well out of harm's way in the knowledge that his brother would assist Henry when he had the opportunity; and whatever his personal involvement (or lack of it) he was still given some of the lands of the Harringtons and other vanquished Ricardians, and the title of Earl of Derby. He had held aloof from Blore Heath a quarter of a century earlier without jeopardising his prospects, and may well have done the same now.

Henry Percy, fourth Earl of Northumberland may seem a strange bed-fellow for Oxford and Stanley in view of his family's long-standing rivalry with the younger branch of the Nevilles, but Eleanor, his grandmother, was the Earl of Salisbury's sister and his role at Bosworth no less critical. Edward IV had rewarded his tacit assistance in 1471 by appointing him to the wardenship of the East and Middle marches towards Scotland and to several other offices in northern England; but he found himself overshadowed by Richard who had inherited Warwick's authority in the region. Their rivalry was restrained by an agreement drawn up in 1474 which effectively defined their respective spheres of influence, and required Northumberland to become Richard's 'faithful servant' in return for an assurance that the Duke would not poach his retainers nor claim any office which he held of the King. They thereafter cooperated amicably, most notably in the Scottish wars of the early 1480s, and Northumberland backed Richard's seizure of power and attended his coronation; but if he expected to be given a free hand in the North once his former rival was established at Westminster he was to be disappointed. Richard continued to maintain his own household and council in the region, and Northumberland would have found his ability to extend his lordship ever more limited. He may have thought that an inexperienced king like Henry would grant him the hegemony that Richard had denied him, and this may be why he brought his forces to Bosworth but failed to engage. Croyland, ever the diplomat, observes that 'in the part [of the field] where the earl of Northumberland was posted, with a large and well-provided body of troops, there was no opposition made, as not a blow was given or received during the battle', but the Burgundian chronicler Molinet states unequivocally that he 'did nothing except to flee, both he and his company, and to abandon King Richard, for he had an undertaking with the earl of Richmond [Tudor], as had some others who deserted him in his need'.[11] He had little choice but to live with Richard while Richard reigned, but would not go out of his way to sustain him or prevent his fall.

We cannot say, at this distance in time, if these three men recognised, or were influenced by, their connections with the younger branch of the Neville family. Stanley's had arguably been severed by the death of his wife at the beginning of the 1470s and Northumberland's grandmother was also long dead, but would they have behaved differently in other circumstances? It was surely King Richard, the son of one Neville and the widower of another, who had first claim on any residual loyalties, but they either felt none or were swayed by other factors. Richard was supported at Bosworth by Lord Maltravers and *his* brother-in-law, the Earl of Lincoln, and by Richard Fitzhugh and his brothers-in-law Francis Lovel and Sir Marmaduke Constable; but their precise roles are unknown, and did not, in any case, affect the outcome.[12] The same is true of the third Earl of Westmoreland, the head of the senior Neville line (who, as 'my Lord Nevyll' had been asked to support Richard's seizure of power two years earlier), the Bergavenny Nevilles, and the seventeen-year-old Richard, Lord Latimer, none of whom were apparently present.[13] There is little here to suggest a common or shared interest, although they might have felt differently if Queen Anne had still been living. Some might have acted more vigorously while others stayed their hands if their loyalty had still been to the Kingmaker's daughter, and Anne's death in March 1485 may have sealed Richard's fate five months later. Perhaps Warwick won in the end.

9

THE SISTERS IN THE REIGN
OF HENRY VII

ichard III's death, and Henry Tudor's accession, were bound
to affect the lives of many members of the aristocracy. Some
were able to serve Henry as they had Richard as though almost
nothing had happened, but the three surviving sisters, Alice,
Katherine and Margaret, all had to adjust to the new situation. Margaret's
fortunes were transformed when her husband led Henry's army to victory,
but Alice and her son Richard would have shared the uncertainty felt by
many who had supported the former government. Katherine's position was
complicated by her son Edward's immaturity and also by the fact that her
husband had been devoted to Edward IV but had met his death at the hands
of King Richard. Dispossessed Lancastrians who had supported Henry
would now expect to recover their former properties, although 'Yorkist'
rivals had held them for some twenty-five years.

The Earl of Oxford replaced the slain John Howard, Duke of Norfolk,
as the dominant power in East Anglia, and he and Margaret were soon
reinstated at Castle Hedingham. They were jointly granted the rich manor
and lordship of the 'Moor' in Hertford and Middlesex (George Neville,

Archbishop of York's former residence in southern England) in January 1486,[1] but their joy would have been tempered by the knowledge that there were still Yorkists who could not, and would not, accept the verdict of Bosworth. One of these was Alice's son-in-law, Francis, Viscount Lovel, who in the aftermath of the battle found sanctuary at St John's Abbey in Colchester. He remained there for approximately six months and almost certainly thought of coming to terms with the new government;[2] but towards Easter 1486 he slipped away northwards and raised a force 'a little beyond the castle of Middleham' that threatened the King when he was at York in April. Henry had few troops with him, but a decisive advance coupled with the promise of pardon for those who surrendered brought him a bloodless victory. Lovel, whom Vergil describes as an 'irresolute fellow',[3] left his followers to throw themselves on the royal mercy and sought refuge with Sir Thomas Broughton, another Ricardian loyalist, at his house on the Lancashire coast.

It is likely that Lovel took the opportunity to visit his mother-in-law, Lady Alice, at her home at West Tanfield as he made his way from Colchester to Middleham. The Fitzhughs had acquired this property when Elizabeth Marmion married Sir Henry Fitzhugh near the beginning of the fifteenth century (the surviving part is still known as the 'Marmion Tower'), and it had previously been used as a 'lady castle', or dower house, by another Elizabeth whose husband, John Marmion, had died while campaigning with John of Gaunt in Spain. Alice probably established herself here after Richard, her eldest son, became Lord of Ravensworth, and may have invited her daughter Anne, Lovel's wife, to live with her before or shortly after March 1486 when Anne's home at Minster Lovel in Oxfordshire was granted to Jasper Tudor, the King's uncle. We do not know if Anne was at West Tanfield when her husband appeared out of the shadows; but she had not seen him since before the battle of Bosworth and they would not meet again for more than a year.[4]

Lovel cannot have remained at West Tanfield for long. Time was of the essence if he was to mount a serious challenge to Henry, and his wife and mother-in-law can have offered him little more than sympathy. The King had recognised that he could not rule the North without the aid of many who had supported his predecessor, and Alice and Anne would have been careful not to compromise their son and brother Richard who had been appointed to major offices in Richmond and Barnard Castle as recently as 25 September. Lovel may have hoped that Richard would cast caution to the wind and throw in his lot with the opposition, but the young man had a great deal to lose.

We do not know how long Lovel hid with Sir Thomas Broughton, but if reports that he was in the Isle of Ely in May are accurate it can have been for no more than a few weeks. Interestingly, it was Margaret, Countess of Oxford, Alice's youngest sister, who took the lead in seeking to apprehend him, principally by writing to John Paston, the recently appointed sheriff of Norfolk and Suffolk. Margaret feared that Lovel would either return to sanctuary or slip abroad if given an opportunity, and Paston was instructed to watch the ports and to 'use all the waies ye can or maie by your wisdom' to frustrate him. 'And,' she added darkly, 'what pleasur ye maie do to the Kings Grace in this matier, I am sure, is not to you unknowen.'[5]

This letter is yet another example of a sister acting with clear, unambiguous authority, presumably because her husband was absent from East Anglia on the King's business. Margaret wrote not as a suppliant but as someone who expected compliance, and clearly put her loyalty to the new government before any personal inclination to help her sister or her sister's son-in-law. Paston would normally have been happy to act on instructions from the wife of his patron, but this time it was not quite so easy. He would have been anxious not to sour his own friendship with Lady Alice (see below), and this may be why Margaret – who may have guessed that he would have to wrestle with his conscience – was so emphatic that he leave no stone unturned. His reply has not survived, and we do not know how diligently he looked for Lovel or excused his inability to catch him. He would have been obliged to go through the motions, but may have been relieved when his 'best efforts' failed.

Francis Lovel remained in England, undetected, until the beginning of January 1487, when he finally slipped away to the court of Edward IV and Richard III's sister Margaret in Burgundy. Margaret was fiercely determined to see a member of her family restored to the English throne (not least because it now seemed to only way of recovering the unpaid part of her dowry), and Lovel brought news of a new, more serious conspiracy being hatched against Henry involving a personable youth named Lambert Simnel. Simnel had been coached to impersonate Edward, Earl of Warwick (the executed Duke of Clarence's son who was then Henry's prisoner) and was already stirring rebellion in Yorkist-leaning Ireland. Lovel persuaded Margaret to hire a force of some 1,500–2,000 professional German and Swiss infantrymen (*landsknechts*), and sailed with them to Dublin in late April or at the beginning of May.

Simnel was crowned king as 'Edward VI' in Christchurch Cathedral on 24 May and his combined Anglo-Irish-German army landed on the coast of Lancashire eleven days later. They doubtless hoped that their arrival would trigger a popular uprising, but were disappointed by the coolness of their reception. Many Englishmen probably feared rather than welcomed a king brought to them on the backs of foreigners,[6] and Henry's marriage to Edward IV's daughter, Elizabeth, had made him acceptable to the majority of the political nation. Lovel and the Earl of Lincoln (who had joined the rebellion in March) decided to try to catch the King off guard by advancing as rapidly as possible; but Henry was ready for them and triumphed on Stoke Field after a hard fought battle lasting some three hours on 16 June.[7]

Francis Lovel was seen swimming his horse over the River Trent in the aftermath of the battle, and presumably escaped. His family believed, indeed probably *knew*, that he had survived the conflict, but rumours that he was in Scotland could not be verified and they were becoming seriously concerned for him by the beginning of 1488. When Alice Fitzhugh wrote to John Paston about some outstanding financial matters in late February, she told him of how Lady Anne had pleaded with the King for Lovel (with little success, apparently), and how his friend Edward Frank had been searching for him in the North. Anne, she said, had made 'great sute and labour' for her husband, and she could not leave her while other friends were urging her to renew her entreaties. Edward Frank had meanwhile returned empty-handed and 'cane nogth understonde wher he [Lovel] is'.[8]

Alice and Anne had made the long journey from Yorkshire so that Anne could seek to make her husband's peace with King Henry, but they were destined to hear no more of him. His fate is a mystery, but Lord Bacon's remark that 'he lived long after in a cave or vault' was apparently confirmed when the skeleton of a man 'as having been sitting at a table' was found immured in a secret chamber at Minster Lovel in 1708. It seems quite possible that he had sought refuge at his former home after the battle of Stoke (Jasper Tudor would hardly have had time to move in – if he ever did – or to change the staff), and died there, perhaps from natural causes or from some misfortune, soon afterwards. His former servants decided to keep his presence a secret – any other course of action would have obliged them to admit that they had harbored a traitor – and Anne and Alice were told nothing. Anne obtained a modest annuity of £10 from the King in 1490, but she never, so far as is known, remarried, although she was still living as late as 1495.[9]

II

The overthrow of the Yorkist dynasty had rescued the Hastings family from Lovel's predatory ambitions, but brought with it the threat that former Lancastrians whose lands King Edward had used to enoble Lord William in the 1460s would demand the restoration of their forfeited properties. William, Viscount Beaumont and Edmund, Lord Roos (whose father, Thomas, had been executed after Hexham) were indeed restored in Henry VII's first parliament and Edward Hastings deprived of much of his inheritance; but such was the weakness of his rivals – and such were the benefits that the Crown might still derive from the Hastings 'connection' – that the Yorkist settlement was by no means reversed. Edmund Roos was simple-minded, unable to play any part in regional government, and Beaumont was persuaded to lease the majority of his Leicestershire and Lincolnshire manors back to Lord Edward for the duration of his (Edward's) lifetime. British Library Harleian Manuscript 3881 contains an agreement dated 2 March 1486 (formulated, we may suppose, with royal approval), in which the newly restored Viscount promised to make Lady Katherine and Lord Edward a 'sufficient and lawfull estate' in a group of properties that included all the Lincolnshire manors held by William Hastings with the exception of his residence of Folkingham, the manors of Whitwick and Markfield in northern Leicestershire, the manor of Edmonton in

Middlesex, an annual rent of £8 from Shepshed (Leicestershire), and the pourparty of the Winchester fee.[10] The Hastings family did not recover Loughborough (which had been seized by King Richard and which the Crown now restored directly to Beaumont), and their interest in Shepshed had been reduced to a moiety; but the settlement gave them the strategic manors of Whitwick and Markfield that had been settled in dower on the sisters' aunt and Beaumont's stepmother, Katherine, Duchess of Norfolk, and who remarkably had survived until at least 1483.[11] Beaumont, for his part, retained an estate that included Folkingham, Loughborough, the residue of Shepshed and the rest of the late Duchess's dower lands, an arrangement entirely compatible with royal policy. Edward IV had preferred to work with powerful, individual noblemen who dominated large areas, but Henry feared potentially over-mighty subjects and opted for a strategy of 'divide and rule'.

This neat balance of interests, the reconciliation of the old Lancastrian with the son of one of the foremost Yorkists, was probably intended to imbue the gentry of the eastern Midlands with the prevailing spirit of compromise; but unfortunately for Henry, Beaumont shortly afterwards succumbed to a protracted mental illness that effectively removed him from the political scene. He was formally placed under restraint on 9 November 1487 on the grounds that he had 'aliened, wasted, spoiled, and put away, great part (of his lyvelode) ... to the disinheritaunce of him and his heires ... and by all likelihode, if he shuld have his libertie therof, would herafter demeane the residue',[12] and in the following March the King granted his 'rule disposition and keeping' to the Earl of Oxford in whose custody he lived quietly until his death in 1508.[13] It is interesting that as late as 1505 the King claimed that a group of properties that included Barrow on Soar in Leicestershire and Leighfield in Rutland (which the Hastings family had held for more than four decades), together with Edmonton in Middlesex and five Lincolnshire manors that had been included in the lease-back agreement, belonged to the Crown as trustee for Beaumont, and obliged Lord Edward to pay £1,000 for permission to retain Barrow and Leighfield in fee simple and preserve his life interest in the others.[14] Edward and Katherine may have contrived to keep Barrow and Leighfield or may have taken advantage of Beaumont's incapacity to recover more of the lands held by their father and husband,[15] but it is remarkable (or perhaps not so remarkable) that it took Henry almost twenty years to 'discover' their fault. Royal clerks sometimes combed the records to unearth irregularities[16] and Henry, secure on his throne, could deal with the parties in a way that would not have been possible in 1485.

Lady Katherine Hastings was conjoined with Edward in the lease-back agreement because he was then, legally, a minor, but she also had a personal interest in recovering the Beaumont properties since three of them, the Lincolnshire manors of Welbourn and Aslackby together with Edmonton in Middlesex, had been included in the provision that her husband had made for her widowhood under the terms of an enfeoffment to use.[17] Lord William had, at an unknown date, conveyed a number of his properties (including, also, the manors of Kirby Muxloe, Lubbesthorpe, Braunstone, Bagworth and Thornton in Leicestershire, and the former Roos manors of Stoke Daubeney, Wilbarston and Sutton Bassett in Northamptonshire) to a group of feoffees (or trustees), and then bequeathed them to Lady Katherine for her lifetime provided always that she did not remarry.[18] They replaced an earlier provision in which she agreed to release her life interest in another parcel of lands so that his executors could apply their profits to the payment of his debts, expenses and legacies;[19] but Edmund Roos had been restored in the meantime and the alienation had lost some of its former value. The balance was redressed in July 1488 when Lord Edward 'desired' the trustees to grant his mother the manors of Wistow and Newton Harcourt in Leicestershire, Welford in Northamptonshire and Burton (Hastings) in Warwickshire (that had formed part of the enfeoffment in which she had relinquished her life interest), and gave her his share in the Lincolnshire estates of Uphall (in Rippingale) and Ouseby (in Birthorpe) in March 1493.[20]

Lord Edward had perhaps provided for his mother as well as he could in the circumstances, but two documents indicate that her finances were straightened in the last years of her life. In October 1489 she signed an agreement with her eldest son acknowledging that all Lord William's personal effects had been divided equally between them (as her husband had wished), except for certain items that had been pledged as security for loans they could not afford to redeem at present. These included a nouche, or ouche (a clasp or brooch), 'with iij diemauntes [diamonds] and vj perlys' and 'a crosse of dyemauntes with a gret perle' (which, with two smaller items, had been pawned to raise £220), together with a ring, crosses, silver and gilt pots and bowls, and 'a coller of Kyng Edwardes lyverey', worth £360 in total.[21] They had presumably been pledged *after* Lord William's death rather than before it, and although most had been redeemed by the time Katherine made her will late in 1503 she had by no means overcome her financial difficulties.[22] She had thought it prudent to buy the goodwill of the influential Sir Reginald Bray, King Henry's Chancellor of the Duchy of Lancaster, but was obliged to write to him on at least one occasion asking him to excuse her delay in paying his fee. She thanked him for the 'manyfold great kindnesses that it haeth liked you to shew to me and myne att all tymes', and blamed illness (the 'coste and charge of phisike') and the failure of some of her own creditors to pay her on time. She enclosed the sum due with her letter, and asked Bray to continue to be 'singuler good maister' to her son Richard and all her other children. His fee would, she promised, be paid more promptly in future, and in the meantime she would remember him constantly in her prayers.[23]

Katherine's income would probably have been adequate if all her tenants had paid their rents promptly, and her excuses are confirmed by a fragment of an arrears roll that survives for Michaelmas term, 1501. This lists five estates, Heckington in Lincolnshire, Lambley in Nottinghamshire, Dronfield, in Derbyshire, Rutland Forest and the Honour of Winton (the 'Winchester Fee'), and shows that she was owed a total of £23 16s 11d, the worst culprits being Heckington (where five tenants owed £7 16s 5d), and Rutland Forest, where Edward Digby and three others owed £8 13s 4d.[24] These were not crippling debts in themselves, but the document is lost after the entries for the Honour of Winton and we are left to guess how many are missing or if the situation was being replicated from quarter to quarter. Her will shows that she was still living in the grand manner (so far as she was able), but it was a far cry from the days when the family spent £993 17s 6¾d on rebuilding Kirby Muxloe Castle in a little over four years!

Katherine undoubtedly had her fair share of difficulties, but there are indications that her dealings with some individuals were unaffected by her change of fortune. In November 1468 Lord William had leased some land in the parish of St Nicholas in Calais to the mayor, William Raufson, for twenty years, the lessee agreeing to render a goose and a gallon of wine at each renewal. The first term would have expired in November 1488, but a full year and a month before this, in October 1487, Nicholas Boveton, Lady Katherine and Lord Edward's attorney, agreed a similar arrangement with the then mayor, William Bentham.[25] This was only a minor event in the overall scheme of things, but shows that, in some respects at least, life went on normally. A single problem often leaves a greater impression in the record than a dozen matters that go well.

III

There are other glimpses into the sisters' lives in Henry VII's reign, most notably in two letters written by Alice and Margaret. The York House books contain a transcript of a message received from Alice on 30 October 1486 interceding for one John Harrington, presumably the John Harrington who was the city's 'common clerk' for six years between 1484 and 1490.

Harrington had been called a 'Scot', a term of abuse in northern society, by one Thomas Wharf, and had arranged for several notables (including Sir John Aske, Sir John Conyers and Sir Robert Harrington) to confirm to the Council that he was a true Yorkshireman.[26] Alice was clearly happy to add her voice to theirs, and told the city fathers that Harrington had approached her in the Austin Friary in York where he had 'soo demeanyd hyme [explained himself] that I and my saide sone [Richard] and all other my sones was verey wele content with hyme'. He was now 'in more singular favour with us then ever he was before this', and they should make this clear to anyone who implied he was not.[27] Interestingly, it was Alice who took the lead in writing to the mayor and aldermen, although her son Lord Richard was now in his late twenties and a significant figure in northern society. Her letters, which also included the missive she sent to John Paston sixteen months later, undoubtedly formed part of a much larger correspondence, and it is regrettable that only two of them survive.

Alice was now in her fifties but remained active in both mind and body. It is likely that she helped to supervise her year-old grandson George after Richard died prematurely in November 1487, and was still fostering her family's interests when she played a leading role in securing a suitable bride for John Parr, her daughter Elizabeth's youngest son, ten years later. Henry Vere of Great Addington (Northamptonshire), who had fought with Henry Tudor at Bosworth, had died in May 1493 leaving four young daughters and co-heiresses, Elizabeth, Amy, Constance and Audrey. The King granted their wardship to William Felde, 'clerk' in December 1495, and he turned a profit by selling Constance's marriage (together with custody of her share of the inheritance) to Alice eighteen months later. We do not know why Alice chose Constance as a bride rather than one of her sisters, but it was not because she was the same age as her grandson. Constance who was said to be 'eleven and more' in July 1502, had been married 'long before' March 1499 when she was probably still months short of her eighth birthday, whereas John, whose father Sir William Parr had died in 1484, was at least fifteen and possibly a year or two older. Nevertheless, whatever the reason, it was Alice who arranged the young couple's wedding at 'Harowdon' (Great Harrowden, near Kettering, in Northamptonshire), after what must have been another long journey from North Yorkshire.[28] Elizabeth Fitzhugh had married Sir Nicholas Vaux of Great Harrowden after the death of her first husband, and John was evidently living with her in her new home.

Margaret's correspondence, like Alice's, is only preserved in other collections, and the *Paston Letters* contain an example of her concern for an old family servant, John Malpass. Like Alice, she calls John Paston her 'right trusty and hertely wilbilovede sone' (sic), although there is no evidence of any relationship between them, and tells him that Malpass 'hath purchacede a writt directede to you and othre Justices of Peace in the shires of Norffolk and Suffolk, and also to the Sheryff of the same, for to put hym in pessible [peaceable] possescion in such certayn landes of his, accordynge to the Kynges writt. I pray you therefor hertely' she continues, 'and of my blyssynge charche [charge] you that at this my pour request and desir ye wole pute you in your faythfull devoir [duty] with othere Justaces associete with you, to see the execuscion doon and performyede accordynge to the saide writt.'[29]

The year is not noted and there is no reference to a contemporary event that would allow us to date the letter with reasonable accuracy; but it must have been written after Oxford recovered his position in East Anglia in 1485 and John Paston was knighted in 1487. Again, we find a petitioner approaching the Countess rather than the Earl himself, and finding her willing to use her position and influence to secure him a measure of justice. Malpass did not, apparently, think he would gain anything by approaching Paston or the other JPs personally, perhaps because he knew that those keeping him out of his lands enjoyed the support of a powerful backer. Good lordship may not have been as crucial now as it had in Henry VI's lawless times, but a polite, firm letter from a lady in Margaret's position would have done no harm at all.

The three sisters who had lived to see Henry VII's triumph at Bosworth survived into the early years of the sixteenth century: Katherine dying at the beginning of 1504, Alice some time after this and Margaret in 1506. By then both the pretender Perkin Warbeck and the Cornish rising against excessive taxation had been successfully dealt with and Edward, Earl of Warwick, the Kingmaker's grandson and the last direct male Yorkist claimant, had gone to the block in 1499. The King's last years were characterised by a growing certainty that the crown he had won would not now be taken from him, and Margaret in particular could console herself with the thought that it was unlikely her husband would again have to 'go on his travels' and leave her in penury. None of them would have forgotten their eldest brother, 'England's Caesar' as he has been dubbed,[30] even though he had been dead for almost thirty-five years as their own lives drew to a conclusion. No contemporary actually referred to them as the 'Kingmaker's sisters', but it was a connection they could never– and perhaps would never – have denied.

10

A Good Ending

edieval people lived with the fear that death could strike
unexpectedly and at any moment, but they did not allow
their concerns to inhibit their pleasures or dissuade them
from striking a hard bargain. Many wrote their wills
only when they reached old age or became seriously ill, perhaps when they
could look back on their lives and seek to make amends for their failings.
It is unclear how many of the sisters left wills – those who died in their
husbands' lifetimes could only have made them with their permission – and
of the three who experienced widowhood (Cecily, Alice and Katherine),
only Katherine's has survived. Dated 22 November 1503, it was proved at
Lambeth on 15 March 1504 and is reproduced, with explanatory notes, in
Appendix 2. Readers can turn to it before or after considering the following
thoughts.

Lady Katherine's first concern was for the well-being of her soul in the
hereafter. She asked to be buried in the Lady chapel of the church of St Helen
at Ashby de la Zouch, and bequeathed twenty shillings and seven surplices
to the church, together with an annuity of £6 to endow a priest, preferably
her own chaplain sir William England, to celebrate requiem mass in the
chapel for three years. The priest was to have the use of a suit of vestments,

her little gilded chalice, a printed mass book and a printed *portvous*, perhaps a collection of litanies. She also left £20 to Lincoln Cathedral, and some lands in Burton Overy and Wigston (Leicestershire), which she had bought from a widow named Elizabeth Kent, to the College of the Annunciation of Our Lady in the Newarke, Leicester, to pray for her and other members of her family on the anniversary of her death forever. These arrangements were not insignificant, but were still a far cry from the hundreds (or even thousands) of masses that some wealthy testators hoped would shorten their time in purgatory. Her limited resources would not run to such gestures, but she did what she could.

Her next priority was to repay the various monies she had borrowed and, in some cases, redeem the pledges she had given for them. Cecily, her daughter by Lord Harrington, was allowed to keep an ornate bed and a gold jewel in lieu of sums outstanding, and Mary, her daughter-in-law (Edward's wife), became the permanent owner of part of a cross. Mary was also left a ring which had first to be redeemed from a William Bamsell, and Edward got a suit of vestments which had been given to the abbot of Darley as security for a loan of £20. William, her youngest son, was bequeathed several items which would first have to be recovered from his aunt Alice (Fitzhugh) and received plate that had been in the hands of one John Holme on condition that he paid the said John £15. Edward was also left an 'owche' (an ornament of gold, or jewels) that had been entrusted to William, an image of Our Lady which was then in Cecily's possession, and a gold salt cellar kept by Mary, while Anne, her daughter by Lord Hastings, was willed a primer that had previously been given to Alice. Katherine had clearly not surrendered her title in these items, but whether they were pledges, or had merely been loaned to the recipients, is unclear.

Her children received other gifts, many of them taking the form of books, clothes and furnishings of a religious nature. Edward was left a primer which his mother had been given by Queen Elizabeth (probably Elizabeth Woodville, Edward IV's wife, or possibly her daughter, Elizabeth of York), various hangings and cloths in the hall and chapel at Ashby, and no fewer than eight cushions, two bearing her late husband's arms and two, curiously, depicting 'imagery of women'. He also gained, among other items, a third of his mother's hay and timber at Kirby, all the bedding she had lately had in London, and was excused a debt of 100 marks. Cecily was left three curtains, six cushions, two carpets and a traverse, or screen, while Anne got five cushions, two cushion covers, two carpets, a cope of golden cloth embroidered with lilies together with an altar frontal, and a 'good featherbed' with a bolster, blankets and sheets.

Edward had inherited what remained of the family estates, Anne was married to the Earl of Shrewsbury and Cecily was a rich widow,[1] so Katherine reserved the bulk of her possessions for her two younger sons, Richard and William. They received, jointly or severally, beds, couches, sheets and blankets, carpets, cushions, hangings, tablecloths, kitchenware, chapel stuff, some armour, all her hay at Lubbesthorpe, the hay at Kirby not bequeathed to Edward, and the residue of her estate including her cattle, rents and arrears. Richard and William were both now in their thirties, and Richard had looked to Reginald Bray to improve his prospects; but there is no evidence that either had married or aspired to a career in government service. Perhaps they needed all the help they could get![2]

Others were not forgotten. George of Shrewsbury, her son-in-law, was left a fine cope of golden cloth of white damask with an embroidered purple vestment; Alice, her elder sister, received a timber bed with a standing cup, and Margaret, the youngest, a pair of silver salt cellars. George, her grandson (Edward's son), inherited a second 'good featherbed' together with a bolster, sheets and blankets, while her two nieces, Lord Hastings's sisters' children, also received bedding and 'one of my finest gowns' each. Other gowns were left to her gentlewomen and female attendants (an 'old' one was earmarked for the presumably retired 'Mother Cecill of Leicester'), while two male servants, John Hudson and Richard Twhytull, received enough cloth to dress as grooms. All her household staff were to be paid their wages up to Christmas (even if she died sooner) and each gentleman was also to have a mark (13s 4d), each yeoman 10s, and each groom half a mark (6s 8d). John Lolls, who may have been her steward, received the generous legacy of £20, her doctor, Dr Christopherson, got a fine black gown and 'one of my best horses', and sir Christopher Hayward, who was clearly a favoured second chaplain, was bequeathed a vestment of crimson velvet with a cross of black cloth of gold. He also received all the fruit that had grown on her farm at Kirby, the tithes and profits accruing to it, and 53s 4d in money to 'content himself for the rent of the said farm' and pay the vicar of Kirby his wages to the following 25 March.

Katherine appointed her three sons, her son-in-law and more unusually, her two daughters her executors, specifying that Edward and Cecily be given first refusal on any hangings and bedding sold to pay her debts and perform her will on condition that they paid as much – and as promptly – for them as anyone else would! Their first task would have been to surrender their mother's personal seal pursuant to obtaining letters of administration and a grant of probate, before beginning the process of settling debts, redeeming pledges, and placing bequests in the hands of legatees. This is not a particularly long or complex will by contemporary standards, but fulfilling it would have emphasised the difficulties inherent in communicating with others – executors and beneficiaries – over considerable distances. It would be some time, perhaps a long time, before everything was settled and letters of dismissal could be issued. One hopes that 'Mother Cecill' got her old gown!

Jennifer Ward warns against taking wills too literally since, she observes, 'they were usually dictated, and it is impossible to know whether the clerk altered or embellished what the woman wanted to say'.[3] This may well have been true in some cases, but the overwhelming feeling here is that Katherine still had everything at her fingertips. She was clearly working from inventories and the sickness she mentioned in her letter to Bray could have worsened; but there seems little doubt that this is an occasion when one of the sisters speaks directly to us and tells us something of her attitudes and where her interests and concerns lay.

Katherine had few lands to bequeath since her dowers from her two husbands would automatically return to their heirs on her passing; but it is worth noting that the Hastings properties had been 'encumbered' by her notional third for more than twenty years, and the Harrington inheritance for some forty-three! Similarly, she had only a small amount of personal jewellery to leave, and nothing in the way of plate or tableware. The reason is that these would have been regarded as family heirlooms, to be handed down to each Lord and Lady Hastings from generation to generation, and it is likely that Katherine had surrendered them when Edward came of age in 1487. Many of the ornaments that she had worn in her second husband's lifetime would have been transferred to Mary, Lady Hungerford, her daughter-in-law, and may explain – in one way or another – why Mary was left only a ring and the part of a cross noticed above.

One of the curiosities of the will is the number of beds mentioned (fifteen in total, including three couches), although seats and tables are entirely absent. Were these, perhaps, the beds the individual legatees usually slept on when they resided at, or visited, Ashby Castle and were they regarded as essentially personal items, whereas tables for example could be used by anyone? Katherine also owned what seems to be an unusually large number of religious artefacts, two copes, seven suits of vestments, seven surplices, seven mass books and primers, two crosses, eight altar frontals and hangings (including three 'super altars'), a chalice and an image of Our Lady. We suggested in Chapter Seven that much medieval religious observance was 'mechanical', but these could imply that, like Cecily Neville and Margaret Beaufort, she had become increasingly devout in later life.

Katherine remained conscious of her own position in society, and 'keeping up appearances' must have added to her financial worries. She retained a number of 'ladies', together with gentlemen, yeomen (of the household), and grooms, far fewer, no doubt, than the sixteen 'gentlemen' (including three knights), forty-eight yeomen and twenty-seven grooms who accompanied John, Lord Howard on a visit to London in January 1467,[4] but still enough to place a strain on her limited resources. It is surely significant that she left instructions that these people should receive 'all such wages that has been unpaid due unto them', and we can only speculate how many of their payments were in arrears and by how much. One thing we can deduce is that if Katherine made her will in late November and asked that her staff be paid until Christmas she did not expect to live even that long – but she did not die until early the next year.

II

Medieval people were not usually noted for their longevity – forty was a reasonable lifespan for a peasant farmer and fifty for a member of the aristocracy – but the sisters seem to have done rather well in this respect. True, Cecily died in her mid-twenties and Joan and Eleanor in their mid- to late thirties; but Katherine and Margaret would have been well into their sixties when they passed away and Alice not far short of seventy. Of their husbands, only Duke Henry and Lord Harrington, who was killed in battle, died while still in their youth. The Earl of Worcester was forty-three and Lord Hastings ten years older when they paid the ultimate penalty, and would probably have lived as long as their remaining brothers-in-law in other circumstances. Lord Fitzhugh was also about forty-three when he died in 1472, but the Earls of Arundel and Oxford and Lord Stanley all survived into their early seventies. Edward IV, the longest lived of the Duke of York's brood of sons, died aged only forty and Richard Woodville, the fifth and last of Queen Elizabeth Woodville's brothers, was still aged only forty-something when he expired in 1491. War and politics had accounted for a good many of their siblings, but the others were only middle-aged when they died in their beds.

The sisters and their husbands almost certainly discussed where they wished to be buried, and would have decided on a particular place, usually the family mausoleum, often many years before their decease. Joan, Cecily and Margaret were interred with their husbands in the Fitzalan Chapel adjoining St Nicholas's Church near Arundel Castle, the Lady Chapel of Tewkesbury Abbey and before the altar of the Lady Chapel of Colne Priory in Essex respectively, while Alice probably chose to lie with Lord Henry and his Fitzhugh ancestors at Jervaulx Abbey (Yorkshire).[5] Eleanor was buried in St James's Church, Garlickhithe, in London, where John Stow noted her grave in the course of his 1605 survey, rather than with the Stanleys at Burscough Priory in Lancashire (presumably because she died at 'Derby House', the family's home in the city)[6] and Katherine, as we have seen, asked to be laid to rest in the Lady Chapel of the parish church of St Helen at Ashby in Leicestershire and not with Lord Hastings in St George's Chapel, Windsor. Hastings and King Edward had wanted to be as close in death as they had been in life, and the implication was presumably that both their wives would eventually join them. But the option of being buried in a royal church may no longer have been open to Katherine when she died well into the reign of Henry VII.

Funerary instructions were often very detailed – W.E. Hampton notes that those given in Lord Stanley's will were of great assistance to the excavators of Burscough[7] – and included the form the tomb was to take and the precise appearance of the effigies. Usually, these would portray the deceased in the prime of life, although occasionally a cadaver was placed beneath the adorned lifelike figure. Their purpose was to ensure that they were not forgotten, a wish that may have owed something to vanity but was, again, concerned mainly with the prayers of the faithful. People who saw the effigies would be reminded to pray for the souls of the deceased in purgatory, and it was for this reason that many noblemen and women who preferred to worship in their private household chapels during their lifetimes chose to be buried in busier places, parish or abbey churches, after their deaths.

The sisters would have assumed that their tombs would endure and they would be remembered until the Day of Judgment, but even the best laid plans could go awry. There would have been changes even if the Dissolution and the Puritans had not damaged so much of the religious fabric of medieval England, and today, only Joan lies in the place she intended and beneath an effigy that has survived more or less unscathed. Neither Cecily nor John Tiptoft, her second husband, are buried at Ely where the latter's nieces erected monuments in their memory, and it is unlikely that Eleanor was reinterred under the now battered image that once graced Burscough Priory.[8] There is no evidence that a memorial was built over Alice's grave or that Katherine's family funded a monument after she was buried at Ashby. Time has not obliterated the slightly earlier 'pilgrim monument' (said to represent William, Lord Hastings's youngest brother, Thomas) or the magnificent mid-Tudor effigies of the second Earl and Countess of Huntingdon, and Lord Edward and his family may have preferred to avoid the expense! The Earl of Oxford asked to be buried with Margaret in Colne Priory where they were both portrayed in alabaster, his feet resting on a stag and hers on a winged boar. The sculptures were destroyed c.1730, but fortunately not before Daniel King had drawn them in 1653.

No record of any of the sisters' funerals has survived, but we do have an account of the burial of the Earl of Oxford, which took place only seven years after Margaret's own death. It is likely that the arrangements made by their executors would have differed only in respect of the Earl's personal status (i.e., the essentially military nature of his title), and would have mirrored the obsequies observed for her siblings at other times and in other places. First of all, Oxford's body was 'ceared' (wrapped in waxed cloth), 'and leaded, and so layd in a coffine of wood and remayned in his chamber twelve days'. It was then placed in the chapel of Hedingham Castle, where priests sang a requiem mass daily and where it was ceremonially guarded day and night by a gentleman usher and ten yeomen of the household wearing black gowns and hoods. The advent of Easter delayed the next stage of the proceedings, and it was not until the 22 April (Oxford had died on 10 March), that the corpse was taken to the parish church in a horse-drawn 'chere' covered with black velvet and decorated with his arms. It was accompanied by six mounted gentlemen (the pall bearers), four others carrying banners depicting saints, clergy, household officers, the official mourners, gentlemen bearing the Earl's standard, helm, crest, and coat of arms, together with 'all the knights, esquires and yeomen of the country and all lords' and gentlemen's servants'. 'Nine hundred and more' black gowns were issued, so the party must have numbered about a thousand in all.

After a solemn dirge had been sung and various persons assigned to guard the bier overnight, the majority of the mourners returned to the castle. They returned the following morning to hear requiem mass and to make their offerings, before again repairing to the castle for dinner. Replete, they were back by one o'clock, and accompanied the 'chair' the 8 miles to Colne Priory where the Earl was to be buried. The priory church had been hung and draped with black cloth decorated with heraldic symbols, and after the Bishop of Norwich and the Abbot of Colne had censed the body at the entrance, the pall-bearers carried it to a specially adorned catafalque. Another dirge was sung, and then 'the mourner's executors and other noblemen went to the place where supper was ordayned'.

Next morning, the burial party heard the mass of Our Lady and the mass of the Trinity before breakfast, and then returned to the priory church for the mass of Requiem. The Earl's nephew and heir offered the 'mass-penny' (a gold noble), and, in a ceremony reminiscent of the Earl of Salisbury's burial fifty years earlier, senior lay figures presented his coat of arms, shield, sword, helmet and crest to the bishop who gave them to the heir before they were handed to Clarenceaux king of arms and Richmond herald. Then Sir John Gryce, clad in the Earl's armour (except for the helmet), armed with an axe, and riding a black-trapped courser, was led into the choir by two knights and two officers of arms. He delivered the axe, point downwards, to the bishop, who gave it to the heir, point upwards, and was then disarmed, the sexton taking the horse as his payment. The principal mourners made their offerings, and then listened while Dr Canure preached a sermon in which he 'right well declared the great virtues and nobleness that was in the same nobleman'. The Earl's banner was offered, the bishop buried him, and the officials present claimed their fees. The account ends at this point, but it is likely that alms would have been distributed, and the occasion would have concluded with a great banquet at which all the mourners – rich and poor alike – would have been fed.[9]

III

The Kingmaker's sisters' lives span a period of some eighty years, from Joan's birth in 1424 to Margaret's death in 1506. They were years in which one king – or as many as three according to some authorities – died violently,[10] and years in which the declining medieval period gave way to the coming modern era. The Tudors succeeded the Plantagenets, villeinage withered in the century after the 'Great Rebellion', the printing press superseded handwritten manuscripts, and guns began to replace longbows on the battlefield. It is only with hindsight that we can see this, of course, but the sisters must have realized that old certainties were fast disappearing, and that what had once been regarded as a changeless, God-ordained society was changing rapidly. The clock could not be turned back.

The sisters had had their fair share – perhaps more than their fair share – of troubles, but there is nothing to suggest that any of them ever succumbed to a sense of hopelessness. Margaret's fourteen years of penury and the sudden and violent deaths of both Katherine's husbands would have caused some women to despair; but the evidence suggests that they did everything they could to protect their own and their family's interests and to improve their situation. They recognized that they had to stand up for themselves because no one else would, and because weakness or disinterest would have made them open season to anyone who harbored a claim against them. Life was sometimes difficult, but they never forgot their responsibilities to their families and to themselves.

The sisters' surviving letters were written at different times and for very different purposes, but they all display a marked degree of competence and an ability to pitch their tone at the right level. This may owe something to the skills of clerks – we cannot tell if they dictated their correspondence word for word or merely gave their secretaries a general idea of what they wanted to say – but the nuances are essentially personal. Eleanor's letter to Piers Werburton and her instructions relating to the lands disputed by William Flemmyng and Hugh Brethyrton are firm, hinting at sanctions; Margaret's to John Paston are more personal but still authoritative; Alice's to Paston and York are friendly, seeking to use and perhaps develop existing contacts; and Katherine's to Reginald Bray is a straightforward apology. Sadly, no replies exist, but the recipients are unlikely to have disregarded them. Each sister (and the clerk who assisted her) would have chosen words that conveyed her standing and meaning, and clearly expected her correspondent to respond appropriately. If the sisters were ever lax, or failed to live up to expectations, there is no evidence of it here.

The letters we would perhaps most like to have – but which are unfortunately entirely lacking – are those that must have passed between the sisters themselves. It would be reasonable to suppose that some were on better terms than others, but all we can say with any certainty is that Katherine's will suggests that she was closer to Alice than to Margaret. She charged her son William to redeem the pledges that Alice held for various sums advanced to her (evidence that she had turned to Alice rather than to Margaret when she found herself in financial difficulties), and the standing cup and timber bed left to Alice probably exceeded the value of her bequest of 'a payre of little salts of silver and parcell gylt' to Margaret. There is nothing to suggest that Katherine had helped Margaret when she was in trouble in the 1470s, and Margaret may, or may not, have been disposed to aid Katherine after the events of 1483–85 effectively reversed their situations. Their personal relationships were bound to be influenced by their husband's politics, and there were perhaps times when it was prudent not to be seen to be too close to a particular sister; but if there is no evidence that they poured oil on troubled waters, there is none to suggest that they used their influence with their spouses to make matters worse. It is perhaps more likely that their own female network helped to prevent their husbands' social and political relations from collapsing completely on occasion, particularly in the critical years between 1469 and 1471. All in all, they may be said to have been typical women of their class and era, women who, like Margaret Paston at a slightly lower social level, did everything that was expected of them and perhaps more besides.

EPILOGUE

The sisters were all dead by 1506 or shortly afterwards, but this was not quite the end of their story. Cecily's only daughter and Margaret's only son died within their mother's lifetimes, but the others left children whose bloodlines would, with one exception, continue down the generations. The exception was Alice, whose eldest surviving son Richard had died in 1487 and whose grandson, George, lived only until 1512–13. George does not appear to have married or had children, and since his four uncles (Alice's younger sons) had also died childless the Fitzhugh barony fell into abeyance among his surviving aunts and their descendants. Anne had not had any children by Lord Lovel, but her sisters Elizabeth and Alice, who had married Sir William Parr and Sir John Fiennes, were more fortunate. We cannot be sure of some dates, but Alice (senior) had outlived most of her eleven children when she died some time after 1503.[1]

William Fitzalan and Joan's eldest son Thomas, Lord Maltravers, succeeded his father as Earl of Arundel late in 1487 or at the beginning of 1488. We do not know if the old man's death had been hastened by the slaying of his son-in-law, the Earl of Lincoln, at Stoke, a few months earlier, but Thomas deftly avoided involvement in the Simnel rebellion. He did not, apparently, fight for either party at Stoke Field and, in a manner reminiscent of Lord Stanley, continued his career as though nothing had happened. Margaret, his wife, was one of Queen Elizabeth Woodville's numerous sisters and he had accepted Richard III's bounty; but he quickly adapted himself to Henry VII and stood godfather to Henry's firstborn son Prince Arthur in September 1486. He was succeeded at his death by his son William (1524–44) and then by William's son Henry (1544–80) who was destined to be the last direct male heir of the Fitzalans. Henry outlived all his children, but his daughter Mary had married Thomas Howard, the Duke of Norfolk executed for his involvement with Mary, Queen of Scots in 1572, and it was their son Philip, Earl of Surrey (Henry's only grandchild) who became the next Earl of Arundel. The Fitzalan-Howards retain the title to this day.

Thomas, Lord Stanley was created Earl of Derby by Henry VII in 1485 and finally died in his bed in 1504. His eldest son, George, Lord Strange had predeceased him, and it was George's son, Thomas, who succeeded to the earldom and served Henry VIII in various capacities until his own death in 1521. In 1507 he married Anne, Edward, Lord Hastings's daughter, thus reuniting two branches of the Neville family. Their son Edward, the third Earl of Derby (1521–72), was the great grandson of both Eleanor and Katherine, and served both Queen Mary and Queen Elizabeth with equal devotion. George Hastings, Lord Edward's son and Katherine's grandson, was created Earl of Huntingdon by Henry VIII in 1529, some twenty years after he had married Anne Stafford, a daughter of the Duke of Buckingham executed by Richard III. Their son Francis, the second earl, married Catharine, eldest of the two daughters and co-heirs of Henry Pole, Lord Montague, eldest son of Margaret, Countess of Salisbury, who was George, Duke of Clarence's daughter. Francis and Catherine's son Henry, known as the 'Puritan Earl', thus acquired a 'Yorkist' claim to the throne through his mother, a claim which he might have successfully prosecuted if fate or political considerations had turned against the descendants of Henry VII and Henry VIII. The *Complete Peerage* says that his candidacy 'was much in favour with the reformers'.[2]

The Stanley Earls of Derby are still with us despite the seventh Earl's execution in the Civil War (the sporting twelfth Earl founded the 'Derby' in 1780), but the direct succession to the Huntingdon peerage ended with the death of Francis, the tenth and last Hastings to hold the title, in 1789. Dr Michael K. Jones has recently revived the speculation that Edward IV was illegitimate and his heirs not entitled to the Crown, a suggestion which he believes is supported by a document kept in Rouen Cathedral indicating that Richard, Duke of York (Edward's father) could have been absent from the town at the time his son was conceived.[3] There is, unfortunately, no record of the Duke's wife's whereabouts (if she was with him the 'problem' naturally vanishes), but there is still a gentleman living in Australia who is descended from the Hastings family and the Duke of Clarence and who claims (perhaps rather tongue in cheek) to be the rightful king of England! What would the Kingmaker – and his sisters – have made of this?

MEMORIALS OF THE KINGMAKER'S SISTERS

1. *Portraits*

Joan, whose painted Caen stone effigy lies in the Fitzalan Chapel at Arundel, is possibly the only sister whose real likeness has come down to us. She rests with her husband in a fine marble sub-chantry covered with delicately carved Gothic tracery flanked by four thin twisted columns with holes in their tops for candles and containing a small altar at the end of a catafalque-like tomb chest. Both figures are robed with their heads supported by angels and their feet resting on the Fitzalan horse and a griffin. Joan wears a York collar of suns and roses indicating that her effigy was made before August 1485 (over two years before her husband's death),[1] and substantial traces of the original colouring and gilding survive on her robes and headdress. The images were formerly invisible on top of the high tomb chest, but were taken down, cleaned, and resited on a slate slab before the altar in 1982.

No memorials exist for Alice, Katherine and Margaret, and neither Cecily's monument at Ely (Cambridgeshire) nor Eleanor's at Ormskirk (Lancashire) can be identified with certainty. Cecily is very possibly the wife portrayed on the Earl of Worcester's right at Ely, but there is no agreement regarding which of the effigies now at Ormskirk represent Thomas, Lord Stanley and Eleanor.

Thomas, in his will, asked that seven effigies he had 'caused to be made' – of himself, his two wives, his parents, his grandfather and great-grandfather – should lie in particular locations in Burscough Priory, but at least three, and perhaps as many as five, of these were destroyed at the Dissolution. James Bromley, writing in 1906, believed that the surviving couples were the first and third Earls of Derby and their wives, but F.A. Bailey argued in 1949 that two of the figures represented Thomas, first Lord Stanley (d. 1459) and his wife Jane Goushill, our Thomas's father and mother.[2] The church guidebook identifies them as Thomas, Eleanor, Margaret Beaufort (Thomas's second wife) and the third Earl, who arranged for the older figures to be brought to Ormskirk. Margaret, who was Countess of both Richmond and Derby, was buried in a magnificent tomb in her son Henry VII's chapel at Westminster in 1509. She could be the lady wearing the coronet, but later countesses cannot be ruled out. It has been suggested that there was once a *bronze* effigy of our Thomas in Ormskirk Church, but if one did exist it was almost certainly made for his grandson, the second Earl, in 1509. The figures appear to have been undamaged when Sir William Dugdale drew them in 1664. Curiously, both gentlemen are shown bearded, an unusual feature and one which might, conceivably, be artistic licence on Sir William's part.

Cecily is also portrayed as a weeper on the tomb of her father-in-law, Richard Beauchamp, Earl of Warwick, in St Mary's Church, Warwick, together with the three other parties to the double wedding of 1436: her first husband Henry, her brother Richard, and her sister-in-law Anne. The figures are carefully executed but may or may not be authentic – the Kingmaker looks considerably older than a man approaching thirty, his age when the monument was being constructed in the 1450s. Henry, Richard and Anne are also portrayed in the *Rous Roll*, a series of illustrated biographies of the Earls and Countesses of Warwick written, and possibly also drawn, by John Rous, a chantry priest at Guy's Cliff in Warwickshire, in Richard III's reign, and in the *Beauchamp Pageant*, an illustrated life of Earl Richard Beauchamp produced by an unknown artist at about the same time.[3] Rous's portraits are stylised, as flattering as the myopic text that accompanies them; those in the *Pageant* are altogether superior and more lifelike. Cecily ought to feature in both works as the wife of Duke Henry; but Henry stands beside his infant daughter in the *Rous Roll* and is coupled with his sister (and eventual heiress) in the *Pageant*. Perhaps some indication of Margaret's appearance can be gleaned from Daniel King's drawing of her effigy at Colne.

2. *Buildings*

Some of the homes in which the sisters lived – Lathom, Hanley Castle, Ravensworth and Great Eversden[4] – have almost, or entirely, vanished, but they would all have known Middleham Castle in Yorkshire when they were children. Both Ralph, first Earl of Westmoreland and Richard, Earl of Salisbury added substantially to the existing buildings, and the girls would have easily found their way around the partially ruined fortress we see today.

The Norman keep at Castle Hedingham was built about 1140 and is among the most magnificent and best preserved in Europe. Margaret's husband added a red brick tower to the west, plus a chapel, hall bakehouse, kitchen and pantries, but his fine bridge spanning the dry moat is now the only major survival from this period. Warwick Castle was built in the second half of the fourteenth century, and much of what remains would have been familiar to Duchess Cecily. Her brother, Richard, made few alterations in the twenty years he held the earldom, but his daughters' husbands, George of Clarence and Richard of Gloucester, added the shorter 'Clarence' and 'Bear' towers flanking a postern (or 'back') gate allowing access to the town.

Arundel Castle was badly damaged in the Civil War and there has been much reconstruction; but Joan would still recognise the twin barbican towers built at the end of the thirteenth century together with the Norman keep and inner gateway. One change that would surprise her is that the Roman Catholic Fitzalan Chapel and the (Protestant) parish church of St Nicholas are now entirely separate, although one is architecturally the chancel of the other. Ashby Castle was also slighted after being held for the King against Cromwell, but Katherine would have known all of the present buildings, not least the chapel and magnificent Hastings tower built by her husband, Lord William.

There are others, of course. We have noted Alice's association with the Marmion Tower at West Tanfield, and it has been suggested that Katherine may have similarly used the completed buildings at Kirby Muxloe as a 'lady castle'. Five centuries have severely damaged much of this heritage, but we can still walk where the sisters walked, and see, or visualise, much of what they would have seen.

WILL OF LADY KATHERINE HASTINGS

22 NOVEMBER 1503

with notes

This was first printed by John Nichols in *The History and Antiquities of the County of Leicester*, 4 vols. (1795–1811) iii, pp. 572–3, and by Sir Nicholas Harris Nicolas in *Testamenta Vetusta*, vol. 2 (1826) pp. 450–6, although see also the amendments noted by John Harley in *Report on the Manuscripts of the late Reginald Rawdon Hastings of The Manor House, Ashby de la Zouch*, Historical Manuscripts Commission, 78, vol. 1 (1928) p. 306.

In the following transcription redundant or missing words that can be replaced by a single modern equivalent are given in square brackets; those requiring a fuller explanation will be found in the notes.

I Katherine lady Hastings, widow, late the wife of William late lord Hastings, having perfect memory and hole mind, considering that nothing is more certain than death, and therefore at all times willing to be ready unto death, and to look for the time of the coming of the same, in such wise that death stele not upon [me] unprepared; whereunto is required not onely disposition ghostly, but also of such goods as God of his immeasurable goodness hath lent me the use and exercise of; intending, through his special grace, so to passe by these temporalls and momentary goods, that I shall not lose eternal [life]; make, ordaine, and declare, this my testament and last will, in manner and form following: First, I most humbly bequeath my soule to God Almighty, my Redeemer, to our blessed lady St Mary the Virgin, and to all the Company of Heaven; and my body to be buried in our Lady Chappell within the parish church of Ashby de la Zouch, between the image of our Lady and the place assigned for the vicars' grave.[1] Item, for my mortuary,[2] I bequeath according to my custome. Item, I bequeath to the cathedral church of Lincolne twenty pounds. Item, I bequeath to the high altar in the parish church of Ashby abovesaid xxs. Item, I will that a priest be found to sing in the said chappell for my fadyr and my lady my modar, my lord my husband's soules; for my soule, and for all Christian soules, and in special for those soules which I am most bounden to cause to be prayed for, for the space of three years next ensuing after my departing; and the said priest to receive yearly during the said three years for his stipend six pounds: and if my priest, sir William Englonde, be contented to pray for me in the said place, and for the other abovesaid, then I woll that he be admitted to the said service before any other priest: And I bequeath unto the said chappell a suit of vestments of bawdekyn,[3] red and green, and my little gilded chalice, a printed mass-book, and a printed portvous,[4] which I will my said preest have the use of, for the said three years, at the times when he shall be disposed to say his service divine in the said place. Item, I bequeath to the said church of Ashby seaven surples [surplices], to be occupied [kept] and used by the ministers that shall doe service in the said church. Item, I woll that my Masse [book], covered with red velvet, that is occupied in the chappell, be given to a poor church after the direction of myne executors. Item, I woll that the colledge of Newarke of Leicestre[5] have, to them and their successors for ever, all my lands and tenements, with all their appurtenances, in the townes and feilds in Burton Overy and Wigston, in the countie of Leicestre aforesaid, which I lately purchased of Elizabeth Kent, widdow,[6] for a yerely obit, to be kept in the said college, for my lord my fadyr, my lady my moder, my lord my husband, and for me for ever. Item, where I owe unto Cecilie marquesse Dorset[7] certain sumes of money, which I have borrowed of her at diverse times, as appeareth by bills indented thereof made; I woll that the said Cecilie, in full contentation of all such sumes of money as I owe unto her, have my bed of arres [arras], tillor, testor,[8] and counterpane, which she late borrowed of me; and over that I will that she have my tabulet [jewel] of gold that she now hath in her hands for a pledge, and three curtains of blew sarcionett [fine silk], and a traverse of blew sarcionett, and three quishions of counterfeit arres, with imagery of women, a long quishion, and two short, of blew velvet; also two carpets. Item, I bequeath to myne especial good lord George earl of Shrewsbury [her son-in-law] a cope of cloth of gold of white damasce, with torpens[9] cloth of gold and velvet upon velvet. Item, a vestment of purpure [purple] velvet, with a crucifix and images of St Peter and St John embroidered upon that oon [one] of them. Item, I bequeath to my lady of Shrewsbury[10] a cope of cloth of gold with lillyes embroidered, and that oon with the image of the Trinitie, with a frontail for an altar. Item, my Prymar, which is now in the keeping of my lady [Alice] Fitz Hugh; also two cushions of counterfeit arres with imagery of women; a long quishion, and two short, of blew velvet. Item, a long covering for a quishion of purpure velvet, and oon short; also two carpets. Item, I bequeath to my son Edward lord Hastings a suite of vestiments, now being in the hands of the abbot of Darley for a sume of twenty pounds, which suite I will be pledged oute of my proper goods; also an owche,[11] being in the keeping of my son William; also an image of our Lady, now being in the hands of my lady marquesse. Item, a salt [cellar] of gold, being now in the hands of my daughter Mary lady Hungerford [Edward's wife]; alsoe a faire Prymar, which I had by the yefture [gift] of queen Elizabeth. Alsoe where my seyd son oweth unto me for certain charges which I took upon me for his sake an hundred markes, as appeareth by his writing thereof made, I, considering the kinde demeanor of my said son at this time in granting of a certain annuity, remit and pardon unto him the said hundred markes due to me by the bequest of William Strote, in part payment for my debts, and for my servants at the next audit. Alsoe, I bequeath unto my said son two coverings for quishions of counterfeit arres, with imagery of women. Item, two quishions of counterfeit arres with my lord's armes; alsoe two paire of curtaines of green tartarin.[12] Item, two short quishions of tawney velvet; alsoe a long quishion, and short, of crimson velvet; also such pieces of bawdekyn, with a frontaile of cloth of gold of blew sattin, as hath been accustomed to be occupied about the sepulchre of our Lord;[13] alsoe a cloth of bawdekyn, with a frontaile of red bawdekyn for the font. Item, an old hanging of counterfeit arres of Knollys, which now hangeth in the hall; and all such hangyngs of old bawdekyn or lynen paynted as now hang in the chappell, with the altar-clothes and oon super altare [cloth], with oon of the vestiments that now be occupied in the chappell. Alsoe all such pieces of hangings as I have, of blew and better blew, with my lord's armes, with banquyrs and cupboard-clothes[14] of the same sort. Alsoe three barrehides for carriage; and two barrehides for clothe sekks.[15] Also the third part of my hey that is at Kerby [Muxloe], and all such tymber as I have there. Also all the bedding that he hath of mine which late was at London, reserved only two fedurbedds and a cowcher [couch] that I wol Richard my son have, and also two carpets. Item, I bequeath to my sons Richard and William four coverings for quishions with my lord's armys of counterfeit arres. Also two hangings for an aultar, with the twelve Apostles embrodered with gold, with a crucifix and the Salutation of our Lady. Alsoe all the pieces of hangings of verd [green] that now hang in my chamber and in the parlour; alsoe all my stuffe of napree pertaining to the pantree; alsoe two pair of blankets, and two pair of fustians; alsoe four pair of fine sheets; alsoe my stuffe of kitchin, as platters, dishes, sawcers, broaches [spits], potts and pans; alsoe all my hey that is in Lubbeshorp, provided that William have the more part of the hey; alsoe two parts of the hey at Kerby; alsoe two vestiments, oon that hath been accustomed to be occupied in my high house, and oon that's occupyed in the chappell; two Masse-books, two super altars, oon of white to Richard, and oon of jett to William;[16] two corporauxes; alsoe to Richard foure pair of brigaunters; and to William two payre; and to them both thirteen saletts.[17] Item, to my son William all such stuffe of bedding as he hath now in his chamber of mine; that is to say, a seller, tester, and counterpoint of roosemary, a quilt happing [bedcover], a white mantell, a white square happing; a square happing, white and black. Alsoe to my son William all such plate as was in the hands of John Holme, with that he pay unto the said John, at the feast of St Andrew next coming, fifteen pounds, in part payment of a greater sume; and over that to doe such charitable deedes of almes as I have appointed to be done by him. Also I bequeethe to my son William four fedur beds and couchers; and to

Richard two fedur beds that he hath, a coucher that was at London, a coucher that's here, and a fedur bedde. Item, I bequeth unto them all the hangings of saye [silk] which be at Kerbye now, as appeareth by the inventory thereof made; and I woll that William have foure paire of sheets of such sorte as he now occupyeth. Item, to my lady Margaret [de Vere] a payre of little salts of silver and parcell gylt. To my sister [Alice] Fitz Hugh oon of my standing cupps; alsoe a bedd of tymbre; and such pledges as she hath of mine, I woll they be pledged out by William, and he to have them. Item, to my daughter Hungerford my part of a crosse, which she hath in her keeping for a pledge. Item, to my son [grandson] George Hastings a good fedur bedde, a boulster, a pair of blankets, a paire of fustians, and a pair of fine sheets. Item, to my daughter Anne Hastings a good fedurbedd, a boulster, a paire of blankets, a paire of fustians and a payre of fine sheets. Item, to my nephew William Ferrers[18] and to my niece his wife, a fedur bedde, a boulster, a blanket, a chike[19] happing, an old counterpoint, sillor and testor, which they now occupy in their chamber; alsoe four payre of sheets, and oon of my finest gownes. Item, to my lady Mary [Hungerford] a ring, which William Bamsell hath for a pledge, to be pledged out of my goods. Item, to my neece Brokesby,[20] three payre of sheets, and oon of my best gownes: my gownes to be given among my other gentlewomen, and oon to Mrs. Booth, and oon to Margaret Cooke, and oon old gowne to moder Cecill of Leicestre, and oon gown cloth of my groome's livery to Johane Hudson, and oon gowne cloath of my growmy's [groom's] livery to Richard Twhytull. Item, to sir Christopher Hayward, my preest,[21] in monie or stuff, whether he woll, ten marks, towards such chardges of reparations of his chauncell as he shall have. Item, I bequeath to the same sir Christopher Hayward a vestiment of crimson velvet, and the crosse of black cloth of gold. Item, I woll that he entre immediately after my departing into the ferme of Kerby appertaining unto him, and to take all such fruits as have growne this year, with thithes, oblations, and other profits belonging to the said ferme; and over that he to perceive in money fifty-three shillings foure-pence, and to content himself for the rent of the said ferme for this year, and to pay unto the preest of Kerby his full wages unto the Annuntiation of our Lady next coming. Alsoe I woll that my household be fully contented and paid for their whole quarter's wages to be finished at Christmas next, and all such wages that has been unpaid due unto them; and over this I woll that every oon of my gentlemen shall have thirteen shillings four pence [a mark]; and every yeoman ten shillings; and every groom six shillings eight pence. Item, I woll that John Lolls have twenty pounds. Item, I bequethe to Mr. Doctor Christopherson oon of my best horses, also a gowne of my fine black. Item, I woll that such hangings or bedding, as shall be sold for the payment of my debts and performance of my will, be refused of [offered to] my lady marquisse and of my son Edward lord Hastings before they be any parcell to be sold to any other body, so that the said lady marquiss and lord Hastings woll give as muche for the said as any other woll doe, and make as quick payment.[22] The residue of my goods not bequeathed, my debts fully paid, with all my cattall, somes of monie, rents, annuities, debts, and arrearages, which it shall happen to me to have and to be possessed of, or due unto me, by any grant or lawfull meane, at the time of my departing, I woll be equally divided between my sons Richard and William. And for the true execution and performance of this my present testament and last will, I make and ordaine Ceicill marquiss Dorset, widdow, George, earl of Shrewsbury and Anne his wife, my daughter, Edward lord Hastings, Richard Hastings, and William Hastings, esquires, my sons, myne executors; most humbly beseeching and praying them, in the way of charity, to take the peyne and labour for the true performance of the same, as myn special trust is in them.

APPENDIX THREE

THE SISTERS' LETTERS

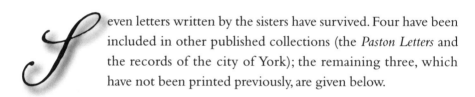even letters written by the sisters have survived. Four have been included in other published collections (the *Paston Letters* and the records of the city of York); the remaining three, which have not been printed previously, are given below.

1. Eleanor, Lady Stanley pacifies a dispute between two squires, 1 May 1466. Source: Lancashire Record Office DDF 600, reproduced with permission.

Aliano[u]r Lady Stanley to all the p[er]sons that theis p[re]sentes shall here or se gretyng For somoche as ther is cont[ro]versie and vanamice [variance] betwene William Flemmyng esquire opon that oon p[ar]ty and Hugh Brethyrton opon [that] othir party for certeyn londes and tenymentes in Longton And [that] the said p[ar]ties byn agreit that suche an indifferent p[er]son as I will apoynt shall have the rule and gov[er]nuance of the said londes and tenymentes and Receyve the fermes and Renttes of the same unto the tyme the said p[ar]ties be agreit and accordet of the title and right of the said londes and ten[emen]tes I therfor certify you that I in [that] p[ar]ty have assignet and apoynted Richard Banastre of the fayrehurst ov[er]seer and Ruler of the said londes and ten[emen]tes And the Rentes and fermes therof yerely at the festes

usuell to take and Receyve opon his due and sufficient accomptes of the same
to be yelden and have gevyn under my signet the first day of May in the yere
of the Regne of Kyng Edward the fourth aftur the conquest the sext

Dorse: An order for sequestration of her possession of s[er]taine landes and
tenements then in question and A[nn]o vj^{to} Edwardi iiij^{ti}

2. Eleanor, Lady Stanley, to Piers Werburton, 27 August 146?. Source: John
Rylands University Library, Arley Charter 30/2. Reproduced by courtesy
of the University Librarian and Director, The John Rylands University
Library, The University of Manchester.

Trusty and welbeloved I grete you wele and forasmuche as I am enformed
that Geffrey Harp[er] of the kynges Eschequier hath an annuytie of vj m[a]rc'
by yere by patent of the lorde of Bergavenny duryng his lyfe with a clause of
distresse in the same in the same And that he is not payde acordynge to his
patent but keped from hym wrongfully by the baillyfe and occupiers of the
lordships of Bromfeld and Yale ... to the will of the seid lorde of Bergavenny
And to grete hurte of the seid Geffrey with oute that he may be content of
his seid annuytie and the arrerage therof which drawyth to the sum[m]e of
xxvj li. As I am enformed wherfore I praye you the p[re]mysses tenderly to
consydre and shewe youre gode will and favo[u]r to the seid Geffrey and
helpe hym to his payement by the nerest meane that ye can acordynge to his
g[ra]unte net lettynge for Fere of any men to execute the effecte of his patent
whiche so done shall cause me to be yo[u]r gode lady in that I can or may by
and kepe you wreten in hast the xxvii day of August.

Aliano[u]r Lady Stanley.

Dorse: To the Right trusty and welbeloved Piers of Werburto[n] esquire
this be delyv[er]ed in hast

3. Katherine, Lady Hastings, to Sir Reginald Bray, 21 February, 1496–1503.
Source: Westminster Abbey Muniments, 16066, transcribed by Elizabeth
Nokes, reproduced by courtesy of the Dean and Chapter of Westminster.

Right worshipful and myn interlie [entirely] wellbiloved cousyn in the moost
hertie maner that I can I recommend me unto you right hertely thenking you

for your manyfold great kindnesses that it haeth liked you to shew to me and myne att all tymes, beseching yow of contynaunce of the same. And where I have been so longe in yowre debt for your fee I besech you thenk [think] noone unkindesse in me therefore for the cause oonly was my great disease of seknes which I have had many a daie to my greate coste and charge of phisike beside odre [other] many great charges. And more over such paymentes were appoynted to have been paied unto me att certayn daies I receyved tham not to my great hevynesse bicause I brake therthorough my daies of paymentes of certain dettes and most specially of your fee which ye shall receyve att this tyme by the berer. And after this tyme I trust itt shallbe paied aboute that daie att which it shallbe due. And where it hath pleased you to bee singuler good maister to my son Richard I right hertelie thank you beseching you to contynew the same good maist'ship towardes hym and all myne children and ye shallbe sure to have of me a trew bedeswoman during my life with the grace of god who have you in his blissed keeping and send you good lyfe and longe. At Asheby the xxi^st daie of februarye.

Sir bicause ye have att all times loked upon my matiere with great favor and been good cousyn unto me and beyn good maister to all my childern in all their causes, and I therefore consideryng that I cowth [can] not recompense your goodness by odre [other] meanes have praied for you by name in good faith and doo and shall doo while my lyfe shall endur, and cause also bett' than I am to doo the same as I have good cause to doo.

Your hertely loving cousyn Kathryn Hastinges

The Kingmaker's Sisters in the Fifteenth and Early Sixteenth Centuries

Henry Bolingbroke deposes Richard II with the help of Ralph Neville, Earl of Westmoreland (the sisters' grandfather) and becomes king as Henry IV.

Birth of Richard Neville the elder, Earl Ralph's eldest son by his second marriage to Joan Beaufort and the sisters' father.

Henry IV crushes rebellions led by the Percies (1403) and by the Duke of Norfolk and Archbishop Scrope (1405) with Earl Ralph's assistance, but suffers increasingly from ill health in the latter part of his reign.

1413

Henry IV dies on 20 March, and is succeeded by Henry V, his eldest son.

1413–1422

Henry V resumes the Hundred Years' War and defeats the French at Agincourt (25 October 1415), but leaves only a nine-month-old infant, Henry VI, to succeed him when he dies prematurely on 31 August 1422.

1421

Richard Neville the elder marries Alice Montacute, heiress to the earldom of Salisbury before 12 February. Joan, their first child, is born before 2 November 1424.

1424

Henry V's brother, the Duke of Bedford, defeats the French at Verneuil on 17 August.

1425

Ralph Neville, Earl of Westmoreland, dies on 21 October and is succeeded by his grandson (the son of the eldest son of his first marriage), another Ralph.

1428

Richard Neville the younger, the Salisburys' eldest son and the future 'Kingmaker', is born on 22 November, a year or two after his second sister, Cecily.

1429

Joan of Arc relieves Orléans on 28 April, and the tide of war turns against the English.

1430s

The Salisburys' younger sons, Thomas, John and George, are all born by 1432. Three more sisters, Eleanor, Alice and Katherine, arrive during the decade, followed by Margaret after 1442.

1431

Joan of Arc is burned as a witch at Rouen on 30 May.

1435

England's ally, the Duke of Burgundy, returns to his allegiance as a peer of France at the September Congress of Arras, seriously undermining the war effort.

1436

Richard Neville the younger and his sister Cecily are married to Henry and Anne Beauchamp, two of the children of the Earl of Warwick, in May.

1438

Joan Neville is married to William Fitzalan, Earl of Arundel, after 17 August.

1445

Henry VI marries the French princess Margaret of Anjou on 23 April, and promises to cede Maine as the price of peace.

1450
_____

The 'peace' arrangement collapses, and the loss of English-controlled Normandy leads to widespread dissatisfaction with the Government. The Duke of Suffolk, one of Henry's principal ministers, is beheaded by a mob (2 May) and Jack Cade's rebels enter London two months later. Cecily Neville, Duchess of Warwick and latterly Countess of Worcester dies on 28 July.

1452
_____

Richard, Duke of York, the leader of the opposition or 'war' party, confronts the King at Dartford, in Kent, at the beginning of March and tries (unsuccessfully) to compel Henry to change his advisors and the direction of his policy.

1453
_____

John Talbot, Earl of Shrewsbury is killed at the battle of Castillon on 17 July, and the English are driven from Bordeaux. Edward, the King and Queen's only son, is born on 13 October.

1454
_____

Eleanor Neville marries Thomas, Lord Stanley, about 17 December. Alice weds Henry, Lord Fitzhugh, and Katherine espouses William, Lord Harrington later in the decade.

1455
_____

The Duke of York, now supported by the Earls of Salisbury and Warwick, confronts Henry at St Albans and again demands reform. When Henry refuses, the first battle of the 'Wars of the Roses' is fought in the town's streets.

1455–60

The Wars continue intermittently, the 'Yorkists' maintaining that their only aim is to secure better government, until the Duke of York dramatically claims the Crown on 25 October 1460. Warwick brokers a compromise naming the Duke as King Henry's successor, but this is wholly unacceptable to Queen Margaret and her son.

1460

The Duke of York is killed at the battle of Wakefield on 30 December, together with the Salisburys' son Thomas and Katherine's husband Lord Harrington. The Earl of Salisbury is executed at Pontefract next day.

1461

Warwick is defeated by Queen Margaret at the second battle of St Albans (17 February) and, in desperation, offers his allegiance to York's son, Edward. Edward defeats the Lancastrians at Towton (Yorkshire) on Palm Sunday (29 March) and reigns as Edward IV, the first king of the House of York.

1462

Katherine Neville marries William, Lord Hastings before February. Joan, Countess of Arundel, her eldest sister, dies before 9 September.

1464

Edward IV secretly marries Elizabeth Woodville, a daughter of Lord Rivers, on 1 May, to the consternation of many of his subjects who expect him to choose a foreign princess who would bring England a dowry and the goodwill of her country. The favour shown to the new Queen's numerous family is one of several factors that undermines the friendship between the Earl of Warwick and the King.

1465 (?)

Margaret Neville, the Kingmaker's youngest sister, is married to John de Vere, Earl of Oxford.

1469

Warwick stirs up Robin of Redesdale's northern rebellion in the autumn and an uprising in Lincolnshire the following March. His success in the former allows him to execute several senior Woodvilles and even hold the King prisoner for a time; but defeat in the latter obliges him to flee to France.

1470

In France, Warwick is reconciled with the deposed Queen Margaret (July) and agrees to invade England on behalf of the House of Lancaster. Edward, deserted by some of his forces (including Warwick's brother, John, Marquess Montagu), is driven into exile in Burgundy on 2 October. Henry VI is brought out of the Tower of London (where he has languished since 1464) and restored as king.

1471

King Edward returns from exile (14 March) and defeats and kills Warwick and Montagu at the battle of Barnet (14 April). He completes his recovery of his kingdom by defeating Queen Margaret and her western Lancastrian army at Tewkesbury on 4 May. King Henry's only son is slain at Tewkesbury, and Henry himself dies mysteriously in the Tower of London soon afterwards.

1472

Death of Eleanor Neville, Lady Stanley. Her widower weds Margaret Beaufort, Henry Tudor's mother.

1475

King Edward invades France in June, but is bought off with a large annual pension and the engagement of his eldest daughter to the Dauphin at the Treaty of Pecquigny.

1478

The King's brother, the Duke of Clarence, is executed on 18 February, although his offences, born of frustration and disappointment, do not appear to warrant the ultimate penalty.

1483

King Edward dies on 9 April at the comparatively early age of forty. His son, Prince Edward, succeeds as Edward V, but the late King's surviving brother, Richard, Duke of Gloucester stages a coup that ensures his own appointment as Protector during the boy's minority. A second coup in June leads to the deposition of Edward V and Gloucester's accession as Richard III.

1483

A rebellion named after King Richard's ally, the Duke of Buckingham, tries unsuccessfully to restore Edward V to the throne in October. The rebels hear a rumour that the young King is no more and transfer their allegiance to Richard's Lancastrian rival, the exiled Henry Tudor. On Christmas Day Henry swears an oath to marry Princess Elizabeth of York (Edward V's sister) when he is able to defeat King Richard, thereby uniting the two rival branches of the royal family.

1485

Henry Tudor invades England with a small force and remarkably, defeats and kills King Richard at the battle of Bosworth (22 August). Henry becomes king as Henry VII and marries Elizabeth of York in January 1486. Prince Arthur, their first son, is born on 20 September.

1487

A group of Yorkist dissidents, including the Earl of Lincoln, one of Richard III's nephews, and Francis, Viscount Lovel, the late King's chamberlain, mount a rebellion against Henry, but are defeated at Stoke by Newark on 16 June.

1491–1499

Perkin Warbeck appears in Ireland claiming to be Prince Richard of York. He resembles Edward IV, his alleged father, behaves plausibly and is recognised by several European heads of state when they wish to make trouble for Henry; but he is unable to say how he escaped from the Tower or name any witnesses who would verify his story. He is captured after the failure of his third abortive invasion of England in 1497 and executed with the Earl of Warwick (the Duke of Clarence's son and the most obvious Yorkist rival to Henry) two years later.

1497

Cornishmen led by Michael Joseph, a blacksmith, Thomas Flamank, a lawyer, and Lord Audley rebel against taxation and march on London but are defeated at Blackheath (17 June).

1501

Prince Arthur is married to the Spanish princess Catherine of Aragon on 14 November.

1502

Prince Arthur dies on 2 April, followed by his mother, Queen Elizabeth of York, in February 1503.

1503

Katherine Neville, Lady Hastings makes her will on 22 November and dies shortly afterwards. Her sister Alice is still living at this date.

1506

Margaret Neville, Countess of Oxford dies after 20 November.

1509

King Henry enjoys greater peace and security after Warbeck's execution, but suffers increasingly from illness. He dies, aged fifty-two, on 21 April and is succeeded by Henry (VIII), his only surviving son.

Notes & References

References are given in full on the first occasion in which they appear in each chapter but in shortened form thereafter. The place of publication is London unless otherwise stated.

Introduction

1   The fullest biographies of Richard Neville are Michael Hicks's *Warwick the Kingmaker* (Oxford, 1998 & 2002) and A.J. Pollard's *Warwick the Kingmaker: Politics, Power and Fame* (2007). Paul Murray Kendall's *Warwick the Kingmaker* is a readable popular life, and C.W. Oman's *Warwick* (1891) a useful short introduction to his career.

2   The Duke of Warwick, the Earls of Oxford and Worcester, and Lords Hastings and Stanley are included in *The Oxford Dictionary of National Biography*, ed. H.C.G. Matthew and B. Harrison, 60 vols (Oxford 2004); some particulars of the Earl of Arundel and Lords Fitzhugh and Harrington may be found in G.E.C. *et al.*, *The Complete Peerage*, 14 vols. (1910–98).

Chapter One: The Rise of the Nevilles

1 K.B. McFarlane, *The Nobility of Later Medieval England* (Oxford, 1973) p. 144.

2 Ralph's most important landholdings were in Durham and Yorkshire, but his title could not conflict with those of the Bishop and Duke of the same names.

3 Quoted by C.W. Oman, *Warwick the Kingmaker* (1891) p. 26, on which this paragraph is based.

4 A child could not be baptised until at least its head had been born, but some theologians conceded that an infant who died in the womb might be sanctified by special privilege of God. Sometimes, parents might contrive to bury a stillborn in consecrated ground secretly, at night.

5 The ceremony is described fully in Nicholas Orme's *Medieval Children* (2003) pp. 27–30.

6 A custom that probably explains why a child was sometimes given the same name as a living sibling, e.g. the two John Pastons.

7 *The Paston Letters 1422–1509*, ed. J. Gairdner, 6 vols. (1904) ii., p. 110.

8 Oman, *Warwick*, p. 28.

9 The secular power was no more decisive. Professor Orme points out that when poll taxes were imposed between 1377 and 1381 the age of liability was set first at fourteen, then sixteen, and finally fifteen. *Medieval Children*, p. 322.

10 Professor Pollard suggests, probably correctly, that Cecily and Worcester connived with Warwick to deliver George's share of the inheritance to him (A.J. Pollard, *Warwick the Kingmaker. Politics, Power and Fame* (2007) p. 20) but Cecily's own part in the 'arrangement' is entirely unknown.

11 John Rous, *The Rous Roll*, with an historical introduction by Charles Ross (Gloucester, 1980) no. 54. *Oxford Dictionary of National Biography*, ed. H.C.G. Matthew and B. Harrison, 60 vols (Oxford 2004) vol. 4, p. 589.

Chapter Two: The Sisters' England

1 J.D. Mackie, *The Earlier Tudors* (Oxford, 1985) p. 25. All quotations from Vergil are taken from this book.

2 *A Relation, or rather a true account of the Island of England ... about the year 1500*, trans. C.A. Sneyd (Camden Society, 1847) p. 20.

3   *Ibid.* p. 10.

4   Mackie, *Earlier Tudors*, p. 37.

5   J. Guy. *Tudor England* (Oxford, 1990) p. 34.

6   *A Relation*, pp. 42–3.

7   There may also have been a seventh in Leicester for most of the sisters'
     lifetimes – the eighteenth-century historian Throsby said that St Michael's
     was demolished 'about 1400', but there is some evidence it survived until
     1490.

8   Mackie, *Earlier Tudors*, p. 43.

9   A. Goodman, *The Wars of the Roses: Military Activity and English Society 1452–
     1497* (1981) pp. 227–8. The first battle of St Albans, fought in the town's
     streets, is the main exception. Warwick the Kingmaker was briefly besieged
     in Coventry in 1471.

10   K.B. McFarlane, *The Nobility of Medieval England* (Oxford, 1980) pp. 148–9.
     T.B. Pugh, 'The Magnates, Knights and Gentry', in *Fifteenth-Century England
     1399–1509*, ed. S.B. Chrimes, C.D. Ross & R.A. Griffiths (Manchester, 1972)
     pp. 88–9.

11   Guy, *Tudor England*, pp. 32–3.

12   *A Relation*, p. 29.

13   *Ibid.* pp. 20–24 (slightly amended).

14   MacFarlane, *Nobility*, pp. 172–5.

15   H.L. Gray. 'Incomes from Land in England in 1436', *English Historical Review*,
     49 (1934).

Chapter Three: The Sisters in the Wars of the Roses c. 1450–1461

1   *Oxford Dictionary of National Biography*, ed. H.C.G. Matthew and B. Harrison,
     60 vols (Oxford 2004) 54, p. 834.

2   W.E. Hampton, Memorials of the Wars of the Roses (Upminster, 1979)
     p. 26.

3   R. Marks, *Gothic: Art for England 1400–1547* (2003) no. 93. The same volume
     includes a description and illustration of Henry's Psalter and Hours (no.
     91) while Lydgate's 'Fall of Princes' is discussed in R.J. Mitchell, *John Tiptoft*
     (1938) pp. 150–1. C.M. Woolgar notes that 'psalters and missals were most
     commonly owned by men, whereas women more frequently owned primars

or books of hours and often bequeathed them to other women'. *The Great Household in Medieval England* (1999) p. 179.

4   C.M. Meale, "'... alle the bokes that I have of latyn, englisch and frensch": Lay Women and their Books in Late Medieval England', in C.M. Meale (ed.) *Women and Literature in Britain 1150–1500* (Cambridge, 1996) p. 145.

5   W.H. St John Hope, 'The Last Testament and Inventory of John de Veer, thirteenth Earl of Oxford', *Archaeologia*, lxvi. (1915) p. 300. Large collections, such as the thousand or so volumes owned by Duke Humphrey of Gloucester, were unusual. Woolgar suggests that 'a few dozen' may have been the norm. *The Great Household*, p. 180.

6   Caxton's Blanchardyn and Eglantine, ed. Leon Kellner (Early English Text Society, 1890) p. 1. quoted by Nicholas Orme, *Medieval Children* (2003) p. 282, on which this paragraph is based.

7   This was no small consideration – see *Calendar of the Patent Rolls, Henry VI, 1446–52*, pp. 37–8. Note how far-flung some of the assets were, and how they ranged from modest rights to large manors. Cecily (and her administrators) would have had their work cut out to identify and collect everything that was due.

8   M. Hicks, *Warwick the Kingmaker* (Oxford, 2002) p. 80.

9   I have here followed Professor Pollard who thinks that anxiety over Wressle may have triggered the open warfare between the two families, but Professor Hicks is more sceptical. He points out that the manor, which Maud might or might not inherit, was never directly fought over, and suggests that it was Salisbury, rather than Thomas Neville, who was the Percies prime target at Heworth. A.J. Pollard, *Warwick the Kingmaker. Politics, Power and Fame* (2007) p. 24. Hicks, *Warwick*, p. 88. Egremont may have been particularly aggrieved because he had been promised Wressle by his father if and when he recovered it.

10   Quoted in Hicks, *Warwick*, p. 87.

11   For a detailed discussion of this see D. Baldwin, *Stoke Field. The Last Battle of the Wars of the Roses* (Barnsley, 2006) p. 7.

12   Although Professor Pollard suspects that the Duke had confided his intentions to Warwick, and that 'it is quite possible' that the latter 'had for some months been party to an elaborate charade'. *Warwick the Kingmaker*, pp. 45–6.

13 He should not be confused with his paternal grandfather and namesake
William Bonville, Lord Bonville, who was executed after the second battle
of St Albans, ostensibly at the behest of the young Prince of Wales.

14 R.A. Griffiths, 'The Sense of Dynasty in the Reign of Henry VI', *King and
Country: England and Wales in the Fifteenth Century* (1991) pp. 89–93, noted in
M. Hicks, *Warwick the Kingmaker* (Oxford, 2002) Chapter 2.

15 Jointure was land held in joint tenancy by a husband and wife for their two
lives.

16 One source says that Elizabeth's eldest son was '13 and more' in 1464,
implying that he been born in 1451. Elizabeth cannot herself have been
born before 1437.

17 Dominic Mancini, *The Usurpation of Richard III*, trans. C.A.J. Armstrong
(Oxford, 1969, reprinted Gloucester, 1984) p. 69.

18 J. Nichols, *The History and Antiquities of the County of Leicester*, 4 vols. (1795–
1811) iii, p. 570.

19 National Archives prob/11/14. St John Hope, 'Last Testament of John de
Veer', p. 277.

Chapter Four: The Sisters in the First Reign of Edward IV

1   The precise sequence of events cannot now be determined, but Lord
Harrington was killed on 30 December 1460, Cecily was said to be aged ten
in 1471 and Katherine had married Lord Hastings by February 1462.

2   Arundel acted as chief butler and constable at Queen Elizabeth Woodville's
coronation and served as a member of the Council while the King was in
France; but these were responsibilities he could hardly have avoided given
his nominally senior rank.

3   Quoted by R.J. Mitchell, *John Tiptoft* (1938) p. 85.

4   John Warkworth, *A Chronicle of the first Thirteen Years of the Reign of King
Edward the Fourth*, ed. J.O. Halliwell (Camden Society, 1939) p. 5.

5   *Ibid.*

6   *The Plumpton Letters and Papers*, ed. J. Kirby (Cambridge, 1996) p. 40. Two other
leading conspirators, Henry Courtenay, heir to the earldom of Devon, and the
late Lord Hungerford's son, Thomas, were executed. Oxford's escape may have
owed more to his Neville relatives than to his willingness to implicate others.

7　　*The Paston Letters A.D. 1422–1509*, ed. J. Gairdner, 6 vols. (1904) iv., p. 300. Gairdner assigns this letter to 1468, but admits that it could be 'a year or two earlier', while Miss Scofield suggests 1469 on the basis that Oxford is known to have been in Canterbury (from where the letter was written) in July of this year. C.L. Scofield, 'The early life of John de Vere, earl of Oxford', *English Historical Review*, xxxix (1914) p. 231.

8　　It is surely significant that Worcester's Neville wife had died thirteen years earlier, whereas Arundel had been a widower for only a few months.

9　　The fact that Stanley left London with Warwick to deal with a Lancastrian insurrection in northern England on 3 June could be taken to imply that he had been present at Bisham, but he could equally have come south in the intervening months.

10　　Surprisingly, Warwick's wife, Anne Beauchamp, does not seem to have been present, nor were his aunts, the Countess of Northumberland and the Duchesses of Buckingham, Norfolk and York.

11　　P.W. Hammond. 'The Funeral of Richard Neville, Earl of Salisbury', *The Ricardian*, vi. (1984) pp. 412–3.

12　　J. Leland, *De Rebus Britannicis Collectanea*, ed. T. Hearne, 6 vols, (Oxford, 1770) vi., p. 2–4.

13　　These scarcer creatures, regarded as delicacies, would have been reserved for the nobles present. Poorer guests would have dined on the oxen and sheep.

14　　P.M. Kendall, *Warwick the Kingmaker* (1957) p. 187.

15　　*Records of the Skinners of London*, ed. J.J. Lambert (1933) p. 81. G.E.C. *et al.*, *The Complete Peerage*, 14 vols. (1910–98) x., p. 243, note i., where the son is called John. It is sometimes said that the Oxfords were childless (e.g. by S.J. Gunn in the *Oxford Dictionary of National Biography*, ed. H.C.G. Matthew and B. Harrison, 60 vols (Oxford 2004) vol. 56, p 308) but this is, presumably, an error unless the Skinners' scribe mistakenly thought that Oxford's brother or nephew (who were both called George) was his son.

16　　Both Joan and Eleanor are said to have had an only daughter, Mary (Fitzalan) and Margaret (Stanley) but others may have been lost from the record. Having said this however, the author remembers that his paternal great-grandfather's first child was an only daughter, and that his six younger children were all sons!

17   The confusion between Margaret and Margery is understandable, and may owe something to the persistence of Norman French in some circles, but how did Beatrix become Joan or vice versa? I am grateful to J.R. Wignall for suggesting to me that she may have taken a new name in religion on becoming a nun.

18   Three of Richard's sisters, Elizabeth, Alice and Margaret (or Margery) married the knights Sir William Parr, Sir John Fiennes, and Sir Marmaduke Constable. Joan and George entered the Church, the latter becoming Dean of Lincoln, but there is no evidence that the other brothers found wealthy brides.

19   The Stanley-Harrington dispute is discussed more fully in D. Baldwin, *Stoke Field. The Last Battle of the Wars of the Roses* (Barnsley, 2006) pp. 30–4.

20   W.E. Hampton, *Memorials of the Wars of the Roses* (Upminster, 1979) p. 100.

21   T. Fuller. *History of the Worthies of England* (1662) p. 109. Hampton says that he was excommunicated and buried 'outside the pale' of his collegiate (i.e. cathedral) church (*Memorials*, p. 100) but these remarks of Fuller's refer to another Lancastrian, Hugh Oldham, who was Bishop of Exeter from 1504 to 1519. The then (second Stanleyan) Earl of Derby was James's nephew, not his brother.

22   Lancashire County Record Office. DDF 600.

23   John Rylands University Library, Arley Charter 30/2. Harper was owed arrears of £26, so had been denied his annuity for the past six and a half years.

24   *Calendar of the Patent Rolls 1461–1467* (1898) p. 382.

Chapter Five: The Sisters and the Wars 1469–71

1   *The Paston Letters 1422–1509*, ed. J. Gairdner, 6 vols (1904) v., p. 63.

2   'Chronicle of the Rebellion in Lincolnshire, 1470', ed. J.G. Nichols, *Camden Miscellany*, vol. 1, (1847) p. 10.

3   John Warkworth, *A Chronicle of the First Thirteen Years of the Reign of King Edward the Fourth*, ed. J.O. Halliwell (Camden Society, 1839) p. 10.

4   P.M. Kendall, *Richard III* (Folio Society, 2005) p. 47.

5   *Historie of the Arrivall of Edward IV... A.D. M.CCCC.LXXI*, ed. J. Bruce (Camden Society, 1838) p. 12.

6   This version in modern English is taken from *The Paston Letters*, ed. Mrs Archer-Hind (Everyman's Library, 2 vols., 1929) ii., pp. 105–6. It is not entirely certain that the letter was written by Oxford as the signature has been deliberately obfuscated, but it does not seem to be applicable to anyone else. Another curiosity is that it is in the handwriting of John Paston III, although he did not accompany the Earl northwards – the most likely explanation is that the Countess showed it to him and he made a copy for himself. See N. Davis (ed), *Paston Letters and Papers of the Fifteenth Century*, 2 vols (Oxford, 1971 & 1976) ii., p. 591.

7   *The Arrivall*, pp. 8–9.

8   More's *History of King Richard III*, ed. J.R. Lumby (Cambridge, 1883) pp. 45 & 51.

9   *Ibid.*, p. 9.

10   M. Hicks, *Warwick the Kingmaker* (Oxford, 2002) p. 213.

11   Sir Henry, who was slain at Edgecote, does not feature in J.W Clay's list of Lord Henry and Lady Alice's children, but the *Great Chronicle* leaves no doubt that he existed. (J.W. Clay, *The Extinct and Dormant Peerages of the Northern Counties of England* (1913), p. 75, *The Great Chronicle of London*, ed. A.H. Thomas & I.D. Thornley (1938, reprinted Gloucester, 1983) p. 209). Sir William Parr negotiated with Edward IV on Warwick's behalf after Losecote Field, but subsequently made his peace with the King.

12   Fitzhugh's rising undoubtedly helped Warwick, but Professor Pollard wonders if a deliberate feint was really part of their strategy. The King lingered in the North for several weeks after the rebels dispersed, and it was only luck that he was still there when the Earl and his friends landed in Devon on 13 September. It is, Pollard notes, 'extremely difficult to coordinate a naval expedition with an uprising behind the lines'. A.J. Pollard, *Warwick the Kingmaker. Politics, Power and Fame* (2007) p. 70.

Chapter Six: The Sisters in the Second Reign of Edward IV

1   *The Paston Letters A.D. 1422–1509*, ed. J. Gairdner, 6 vols. (1904) v., p. 137.

2   *Ibid.*, p. 289.

3   See A. Crawford, 'Victims of attainder; the Howard and de Vere women in the late fifteenth century' in K. Bate and M. Barber, eds., *Medieval Women in*

Southern England, Reading Medieval Studies, vol. 15 (1989).

4   *The Household Books of John Howard, Duke of Norfolk, 1462–1471, 1481–1483*, ed. A. Crawford (Stroud, 1992) II., pp. 100 & 421. It is worth noting that Oxford and Margaret helped Howard's imprisoned son and daughter-in-law when their situations were reversed after 1485.

5   *Calendar of the Patent Rolls 1476–85* (1901) p. 254.

6   *The Paston Letters*, ed. Gairdner, v., pp. 135–6.

7   Ingulph's *Chronicle of the Abbey of Croyland*, trans. H.T. Riley (1854) p. 470.

8   *Ibid.*

9   *The Paston Letters*, ed. Gairdner, v., p. 195.

10 *Materials for a History of the Reign of Henry VII*, ed. W. Campbell, 2 vols (1873–77) ii., pp. 211–2. Henry relented and gave her a life interest in a number of other properties (including Tewkesbury) three years later in December 1490 (*Ibid.*, p. 551).

11 John Rous, *The Rous Roll, with an historical introduction by Charles Ross* (Gloucester, 1980) no. 56. Rous is invariably complimentary, but his comment that she was 'glad to be at and with women that traveld of chyld' rings true.

12 *Calendar of the Patent Rolls, Edward IV 1467–77* (1900) p. 532.

13 *Calendar of the Close Rolls, Edward IV, Edward V, Richard III 1477–85* (1954) p. 76.

14 See his dealings with Katherine Hastings and others discussed in Chapter Eight.

15 W.H. Dunham, 'Lord Hastings' Indentured Retainers, 1461–1483', *Transactions of the Connecticut Academy of Arts and Sciences*, xxxix (New Haven, 1955) pp. 117–8.

16 See Chapter Five.

17 *Cal. Pat. Rolls 1467–77*, pp. 456–7.

18 F.P. Barnard. *Edward IV's French Expedition of 1475* (1925, reprinted Gloucester, 1975) pp. 21–2.

19 *The Memoirs of Philip de Commines*, ed. A.R. Scoble, 2 vols (1856) ii., p. 6.

20 Hastings's master mason, John Couper, made several visits to Lord Cromwell's red and blue brick castle at Tattershall when building with the same materials at Kirby.

Chapter Seven. The Sisters 'At Home'

1 *The Household Book of Dame Alice de Bryene*, trans. M.K. Dale, ed. V.B. Redstone (Suffolk Institute of Archaeology and History, 1984).

2 These are: National Archives, E.368/220 m 107d; Essex Record Office, D/DPr 139, m.1d; *Household Books of John, Duke of Norfolk and Thomas, Earl of Surrey, temp. 1481–1490*, ed. J.P. Collier (Roxburghe Club, 1844); List & Index Society, Special Series, vol. 22, Henry E. Huntington Library Hastings Manuscripts, ed. K. Watson (1987) p. 136, HAM, box 74, folder 7.

3 *Household Books*, pp. 508–9 & 514.

4 W.H. St John Hope, 'The Last Testament and Inventory of John de Veer, thirteenth Earl of Oxford', *Archaeologia*, lxvi. (1915) pp. 282, 285, 293, 328, 330, 332–3.

5 A.F. Sutton and L. Visser-Fuchs with P.W. Hammond, *The Reburial of Richard, Duke of York 21–30 July 1476* (1996) p. 19. *The Great Chronicle of London*, ed. A.H. Thomas & I.D. Thornley (reprinted Gloucester, 1983) p. 207. Ffiona Swabey. *Medieval Gentlewoman* (Stroud, 1999) pp. 151–3.

6 *Report on the Manuscripts of the late Reginald Rawdon Hastings of The Manor House, Ashby de la Zouch*, Historical Manuscripts Commission, 78, vol. 1 (1928) pp. 301–2. Thomas was to marry one of Hastings's nieces if a daughter failed to arrive.

7 Hastings Manuscripts, i. p. 297. Similarly, William Catesby's widow, Margaret, was charged to 'leve sole [live singly] ... all the dayes of your liff' when her husband made his will shortly before his execution after the battle of Bosworth. See D. Williams, 'The hastily drawn up will of William Catesby, esquire, 25 August 1485', *Transactions of the Leicestershire Archaeological and Historical Society* (1975–6) pp. 43–51. The aim was usually to safeguard the heir against the possible ambitions of a second husband, particularly if the widow held lands of her own.

8 The most obvious example is that of Katherine of Valois, Henry V's widow, who bore her Welsh squire Owen Tudor four children without anyone, apparently, finding out.

9 H.S. Bennett, *The Pastons and their England* (Cambridge, 1979) pp. 262–3. The average of 1602 miles covered in forty-six days.

10 C.M. Woolgar, *The Great Household in Medieval England* (1999) p. 187.

11 *The Pastons and their England*, p. 130.

12 Quoted in *The Chronicles of the Wars of the Roses*, ed. E. Hallam (1988) p. 105.

13 There were, even then, 'alternative' therapies such as the recitation of spells invoking the help of Christ or the saints, visiting a saint's grave, or, in cases of scrofula, seeking the royal 'touch'.

14 *Calendar of the Patent Rolls, Edward IV 1467–77* (1900) p. 90.

15 Patrons were not, strictly speaking, obliged to maintain churches since they were usually only responsible for the chancel, but many had little choice but to contribute when large sums were needed. The advantages were that they were able to commemorate both themselves and members of their families, and exercise their right of advowson to 'present' a favoured clerk to the benefice when the opportunity arose.

16 See Ann Wroe, *Perkin. A Story of Deception* (2004) pp. 178–9, for the treasons that were hatched or encouraged within Cecily's circle. Margaret Beaufort's assets in plate, jewels and rich materials alone amounted to £14724. M.K. Jones & M.G. Underwood, *The King's Mother* (Cambridge, 1992) p. 239.

Chapter Eight: The Sisters in the Reign of Richard III

1 Ingulph's *Chronicle of the Abbey of Croyland*, trans. H.T. Riley (1854) p. 488.

2 *The Coronation of Richard III: the Extant Documents*, ed. A.F. Sutton & P.W. Hammond (Gloucester, 1983) pp. 169–70. The paragraphs in this section are all based on this source.

3 Arundel was probably chief butler, a duty he certainly fulfilled at Henry VII's coronation two years later. Curiously, Stanley's eldest son, George, Lord Strange, does not seem to have been present.

4 *British Library Harleian Manuscript 433*, ed. R. Horrox & P.W. Hammond, 4 vols (Upminster & London, 1979–83) ii., pp. 4–5.

5 *Report on the Manuscripts of the late Reginald Rawdon Hastings of The Manor House, Ashby de la Zouch*, Historical Manuscripts Commission, 78, vol. 1 (1928) pp. 3 & 296.

6 K.B. McFarlane, England in the Fifteenth Century (1981) p. 250 and notes 50 & 51.

7   Harley 433, ii., p. 53.

8   British Library Harleian Manuscript 3881, fos. 24 & 24d

9   John Nichols, *The History and Antiquities of the County of Leicester*, 4 vols
     (1795–1811) iii, p. 573.

10   There may be a mistake in the date of course – see S.B. Chrimes, *Henry VII*
     (1984) p. 331. It is clearly at odds with Vergil's assertion that Stanley 'crowned'
     Henry immediately after the battle. Croyland says that only the urgency of
     the moment saved Strange's life.

11   *Croyland Chronicle*, p. 503. M. Bennett, *The Battle of Bosworth* (Stroud, 1997) p.
     161.

12   John de la Pole, Earl of Lincoln, who King Richard may have regarded as his
     preferred successor, had married Margaret Fitzalan, old Arundel's daughter.
     Sir Marmaduke had married Henry and Alice Fitzhugh's daughter Margaret
     (Margery).

13   King Richard's letter to Lord Ralph Nevill (who succeeded his elderly uncle
     as Earl of Westmoreland in 1484) is in *The Paston Letters A.D. 1422–1509*, ed.
     J. Gairdner, 6 vols (1904) vi., pp. 71–2. No source mentions the two George
     Nevilles of Bergavenny, and Richard, Lord Latimer was in the care of his
     great-uncle, the Archbishop of Canterbury.

Chapter Nine: The Sisters in the Reign of Henry VII

1   *Materials for a History of the Reign of Henry VII*, ed. W. Campbell, 2 vols
     (1873–77) i., p. 249.

2   Henry's surprise when he heard that Lovel had left the sanctuary and was
     plotting against him suggests that there had been negotiations and that
     he anticipated a favourable outcome. See D. Baldwin, *The Lost Prince. The
     Survival of Richard of York* (Stroud, 2007) pp. 87–95.

3   *The Anglica Historia of Polydore Vergil, A.D. 1485–1537*, ed. D. Hay (1950)
     p. 11.

4   The last time was probably in June 1487 when 'Lambert Simnel's' rebel
     Yorkist army passed through West Tanfield on its way to the battle of Stoke.

5   *The Paston Letters A.D. 1422–1509*, ed. J. Gairdner, 6 vols. (1904) vi, pp. 92–3.
     The term 'late' refers to the fact that he had been deprived of his title and
     was no longer a lord.

6   G.M. Trevelyan, *A Shortened History of England* (Harmondsworth, 1959) p. 200.

7   For a full account of these events see D. Baldwin, *Stoke Field. The Last Battle of the Wars of the Roses* (Barnsley, 2007).

8   *The Paston Letters*, vi, pp. 91–2. James Gairdner attributed this letter to 1486 when Lovel was in sanctuary at Colchester, but the context seems to support Professor Norman Davis's opinion that it was written in 1488. See N. Davis, *Paston Letters and Papers of the Fifteenth Century*, 2 vols (Oxford 1971–76) ii. pp. 455–6.

9   For a full discussion of the circumstances of Lovel's disappearance see Baldwin, *Stoke Field*, Chapter 7.

10   British Library Harleian Manuscript 3881, fos. 23 & 23d. *Calendar of the Close Rolls 1485–1500* (1954) pp. 16–17.

11   Katherine had survived no fewer than four husbands including William Beaumont's father, John (her third) and the last, John Woodville, who was over forty years her junior!

12   *Rolls of Parliament*, vi (1783) p. 389.

13   *Calendar of the Patent Rolls, Henry VII 1485–1494* (1914) p. 222.

14   *Calendar of the Close Rolls, Henry VII 1500–1509* (1963) pp. 187–8. The 1486 leaseback agreement had been enrolled on the *Close Rolls*, so that, at least, was in no way underhand, and it is impossible to say why Henry chose to make an issue of just five of the Lincolnshire manors included in it in 1505.

15   The situation regarding Barrow would have been complicated by the fact that Lord William had conveyed it to trustees to help provide for his wife's dower in the event of his death.

16   The Croyland writer remarks how Richard III had ordered 'chosen men ... to scrape up immense sums of money after examining the archives of the realm'. Ingulph's *Chronicle of the Abbey of Croyland*, trans. H.T. Riley (1854) p. 498.

17   An enfeoffment was a device often used to circumvent the law of primogeniture – the right of an heir to succeed to all his late father's properties – by conveying a certain part of them to a group of trustees. The trustees became the legal owners, but undertook to distribute them, or utilise the revenues, as the donor had wished.

18   *Report on the Manuscripts of the late Reginald Rawdon Hastings of The Manor House, Ashby de la Zouch*, Historical Manuscripts Commission, 78, vol. I (1928) p. 297.

19   See William Hastings's will in J. Nichols, *The History and Antiquities of the County of Leicester*, 4 vols (1795–1811) iii, pp. 570–1.

20.   Hastings Manuscripts, i., pp. 145 & 297.

21   *Ibid.*, pp. 305–6

22   It is possible that 'my part of a crosse' then in the keeping of Mary, Lady Hungerford, a ring pawned to William Bamsell, and 'such plate as was in the hands of John Holme' were the same as items mentioned in the 1488 agreement, but whether they had been redeemed in the interim and subsequently re-pledged is unknown. Nichols, *History of Leicester*, iii., p. 573.

23   Westminster Abbey Muniments, 16066, transcribed by Elizabeth Nokes. Punctuation added. It has been attributed to the period 1496–1503 – see P. Tudor-Craig, *Richard III* (National Portrait Gallery Exhibition Catalogue, 1973) no. 78.

24   List & Index Society, Special Series, vol. 22, *Henry E. Huntington Library Hastings Manuscripts*, ed. K. Watson (1987) p. 136, HAM Box 74, folder 7. None of the estates mentioned had formed part of her original dower, and Lambley, which was worth £24 in 1507–08, had been specifically bequeathed to her son Richard. An Inquisition Post Mortem held near the end of Henry VII's reign says that Richard 'intruded into', i.e. deprived his mother of, the manor on 20 April 1497, but Katherine had apparently recovered it by 1501 (*Calendar of Inquisitions Post Mortem, Henry VIII, 1504–1509* (1955) no. 476, pp 289–90). She seems to have held Dronfield in her own right (*Ibid.*, no. 575, pp. 345–6).

25   Hastings Manuscripts, i., pp. 273–4. Lord William served as Edward IV's lieutenant at Calais in the 1470s.

26   *York House Books 1461–1490*, ed. L.C. Attreed, 2 vols. (Stroud, 1991) ii., p. 515. The letter has also been printed in R. Davies, *Extracts from the Municipal Records of the City of York during the reigns of Edward IV, Edward V, and Richard III* (1843) pp. 301–2.

27   It is only the context of the other testimonies that allows us to assume that Alice was concerned with the same matter – otherwise the logical

interpretation would be that Harrington had offended her and her son, Lord Richard, personally, but had subsequently apologised or made amends.

28 CIPM, Henry VII 1504–1509, no. 757, p. 408. The wardships of the other three sisters were subsequently acquired by John Mordaunt of Turvey (Beds.) who married two of the girls to two of his own sons. John Parr lived only until 1504 when his bride would have been about twelve.

29 *The Paston Letters*, vi., p. 165.

30 A.J. Pollard, *Warwick the Kingmaker* (2007) Chapter 3, quoting from Antonio della Torre who described the earl as 'like another Caesar in these parts' (p. 49).

Chapter Ten: A Good Ending

1 Her husband, the first Marquess of Dorset, had died in 1501. She married Henry Stafford, Earl of Wiltshire, in 1505, and was still living when the future Queen Elizabeth I was christened in 1533.

2 Lord William had left Richard the manors of Lambley and Bleasby in Nottinghamshire together with Drakenage in Warwickshire, while William received Arnold in Nottinghamshire and Bruntingthorpe, Ashby Parva and Fleckney in Leicestershire, but they never emerge from their elder brother's shadow. J. Nichols, *The History and Antiquities of the County of Leicester*, 4 vols (1795–1811) iii., pp. 570–1.

3 J.C. Ward, *English Noblewomen in the Later Middle Ages* (1992) p. 95.

4 Noted by A.J. Pollard in *Imagining Robin Hood* (Abingdon, 2007) p. 37.

5 There is no record of where Alice chose to be buried. Some parts of Jervaulx Abbey, the Monks' Dorter for example, still stand to a considerable height, but the church has been virtually levelled and only a single badly worn effigy (of an earlier cross-legged knight) survives there. She may have preferred to lie in the church of St Nicholas at West Tanfield (Yorkshire) next to the Marmion Tower where she spent the last years of her life.

6 Derby House, near St Paul's Wharf, was named after the hundred of West Derby in Lancashire which included the family's principal manors of Lathom and Knowsley. It may also be why Lord Thomas was created Earl of Derby in 1485. The present St James's was built by Wren after the Great Fire.

7   W.E. Hampton, *Memorials of the Wars of the Roses* (Upminster, 1979) p. 103.

8   We cannot be certain which of the two female effigies represents Cecily, but other examples suggest that the first, or senior, wife was usually placed on the deceased's right. In the case of the first Earl of Westmoreland's tomb at Staindrop in County Durham, W.H. St John Hope (*Heraldry for Craftsmen and Designers* (1929)) identifies the wife on Ralph's right as Joan Beaufort and the one on his left as Margaret Stafford. Joan was, in fact, the Earl's second wife, but enjoyed greater social precedence: Cecily was both Worcester's first wife and the widow of a Duke.

9   British Library Harleian Manuscript 295, f. 155, transcribed in S.A. Ashhurst Majendie, *Some Account of the Family of De Vere, The Earls of Oxford, and of Hedingham Castle in Essex* (1904) pp. 30–34. I am grateful to John Ashdown Hill for supplying me with a copy of this.

10   Henry VI may, or may not, have been killed in the Tower after the battle of Tewkesbury, and Edward V could have died from natural causes. See D. Baldwin, *The Lost Prince. The Survival of Richard of York* (Stroud, 2007).

Epilogue

1   The likely exceptions are Elizabeth who died before 28 January 1513, and possibly George, who became Rector of Bedale and Dean of Lincoln, and died on 20 November 1505. There is no reference to Anne Lovel in any source after 1495.

2   G.E.C. *et al.*, *The Complete Peerage*, 14 vols (1910–98) vi, p. 657.

3   In *Bosworth 1485. Psychology of a Battle* (Stroud, 2002).

Appendix One: Memorials of the Kingmaker's Sisters

1   The Earl's own effigy could have been partly or wholly made in his lifetime, and Joan's at any time after her death in 1462. A recently discovered indenture shows that the chantry was originally made for Richard Dalyngrygge of Bodiam Castle before being acquired by the Earl's executors. See J.M. Robinson, 'Fitzalan Chapel, Arundel', *Country Life* (May 1, 2008) p. 90.

2   National Archives prob/11/14. N. H. Nicolas, *Testamenta Vetusta*, vol. 2 (1826) pp. 458–60. F.A. Bailey, 'Some Stanley Heraldic Glass from Worden

Hall, Lancashire', *Transactions of the Historic Society of Lancashire and Cheshire,* ci for 1949 (Liverpool, 1950) pp. 70 (note 4) & 76 (note 1).

3   It has been suggested that Rous produced his roll (or rather rolls, since there are parallel English and Latin versions) in anticipation of Richard III's state visit to Warwick in August 1483; the *Pageant* was almost certainly commissioned by the Dowager Countess Anne to commemorate the life of her father, and probably, as Alexandra Sinclair suggests, for the edification and entertainment of her grandson Edward (Richard III's son) who was then heir to the throne. The Kingmaker and his wife are also portrayed in *The Salisbury Roll of Arms*, a work associated with the burial of his parents and brother at Bisham priory in 1463.

4   It is unlikely that the 'several nice timber-framed houses' at Great Eversden mentioned by Pevsner preserve any fragments of the Tiptofts' former manor. N. Pevsner, *The Buildings of England. Cambridgeshire* (1954) p. 318.

Appendix Two: The Will of Lady Katherine Hastings, 22 November 1503

1   The site of the original Lady chapel seems to have been lost at the Reformation, and may not correspond to the present chapel of the same name. There are two vaults beneath St Helen's Church, one under the chancel, and the other, containing older coffins, below the Huntingdon Chapel. They were last accessed after being flooded in the 1960s when a photograph was taken, but no other information seems to have been recorded at the time.

2   A gift claimed by the Church from a deceased person's estate.

3   Oriental cloth woven of silk, shot through with gold (or silver) thread, or brocaded.

4   A portvous may have been a collection of litanies. I am indebted to John Ashdown-Hill for this suggestion.

5   The collegiate church of St Mary in the Newarke, Leicester.

6   Katherine did not complete her purchase of these lands, for which she paid £16 13s 4d, until 1 December 1503, i.e. just over a week after she made her will. They were therefore almost certainly bought for this purpose, perhaps because the College had indicated that it preferred real estate to money. A. Hamilton Thompson. *A Calendar of Charters and Other Documents Belonging*

to the Hospital of William Wyggeston at Leicester (Leicester, 1933) p. 530, no. 1052. I am indebted to J.R. Wignall for this reference.

7   See Chapter Ten, note 1, above.

8   An arras was a tapestry, often used as a screen, or hanging. A testor was a canopy over a bed, a term that could also include the structure that supported it.

9   Damask is a lustrous reversible fabric having a plain background woven with patterns, after the style invented at Damascus. I cannot discover a meaning for 'torpens' in this context – the word is interpreted thus by Nichols and accepted without comment by later writers, but appears to read 'thorphent' in the copy of the will kept at the National Archives. I am grateful to Lesley Boatwright for suggesting that 'for the orpent' may be meant here.

10   Anne, Katherine's daughter by Lord Hastings. It is curious that Katherine refers to her here by her title and later, by her first name, but there is no other possible candidate. Anne's mother-in-law, the previous countess (another Katherine), had died in 1476.

11   An 'owche' (ouche, nouche) was an ornament of gold, or jewels.

12   Tartarin was a rich silken fabric imported from the East, probably from China through 'Tartary'.

13   Perhaps the place where the emblems of bread and wine were reserved in the castle chapel.

14   'Banquyrs' (bankers) were coverings for chairs or benches, usually of tapestry.

15   'Barrehides', or barehides, were hides used as coverings for packages, clothes, etc, after more delicate items had first been placed in cloth 'sacks' or bags.

16   The term *super* altars may refer to altar dressings, perhaps to an antependium (altar frontal) or a dosal (hanging reredos). Alternatively, perhaps an entire set of hangings, antependium, dosal and ridels, may be meant. I am grateful to John Ashdown-Hill for these suggestions.

17   Brigandines (or brigantines) were coats or mail or jackets reinforced with metal plates, while sallets were light helmets with a projection over the back of the neck. I have been unable to discover a precise meaning for 'corporaux', but the context suggests body armour of some kind.

18   William, Lord Hastings's sister, Anne, had married Sir Thomas Ferrers of Tamworth (Staffordshire).

19   This word, rendered as 'chike' by Nichols and others, more closely resembles 'thikke' in the original, and is probably a version of 'tike', a case or cover containing feathers and the like, and forming a mattress or pillow.

20   William, Lord Hastings's sister Joan had married John Brooksby of Frisby (Leicestershire).

21   Hayward was not the parish priest of either Ashby or Kirby – could he have been a second household chaplain who ministered to Katherine when she lived at the latter?

22   Surely a personal interjection, however much of the more routine parts of the will her secretary was writing for her. Edward and Cecily were not to suppose that their special position entitled them to behave more casually than anyone else!

BIBLIOGRAPHY

Manuscript Sources

British Library Harleian Manuscripts 295, 3881.
Essex Record Office. D/DPr 139.
Huntington Library. HAM Box 74(7).
John Rylands University Library, Arley Charter 30/2.
Lancashire County Record Office. DDF 600.
National Archives prob/11/14.
Westminster Abbey Muniments, WAM 16066.

Printed Primary Sources

The Anglica Historia of Polydore Vergil, A.D. 1485–1537, ed. D. Hay (1950).
The Beauchamp Pageant, ed. A. Sinclair (Donington, 2003).
British Library Harleian Manuscript 433, ed. R. Horrox and P.W. Hammond, 4
vols. (1979–83).
Calendar of the Close Rolls, Edward IV, Edward V, Richard III 1476–1485 (1954);
Henry VII 1485–1500 (1955); Henry VII 1500–1509 (1963).

Calendar of Inquisitions Post Mortem, Henry VII 1504–1509 (1955).

Calendar of the Patent Rolls, Henry VI 1446–1452 (1909); *Edward IV 1461–1467* (1898); *1467–1477* (1900); *Edward IV, Edward V, Richard III 1476–1485* (1901); *Henry VII 1485–1494* (1914).

Chronicle of the Rebellion in Lincolnshire, 1470, ed. J.G.Nichols, *Camden Miscellany*, vol. 1, (1847).

The Coronation of Richard III: the Extant Documents, ed. A.F. Sutton & P.W. Hammond (Gloucester, 1983).

The Crowland Chronicle Continuations 1459–1486, ed. N. Pronay & J. Cox (1986).

Edward IV's French Expedition of 1475, ed. F.P. Barnard (1925, reprinted Gloucester, 1975).

The Great Chronicle of London, ed. A.H. Thomas & I.D. Thornley (1938, reprinted Gloucester, 1983).

Historie of the Arrivall of Edward IV... A.D. M.CCCC.LXXI, ed. J. Bruce (Camden Society, 1838).

The Household Book of Dame Alice de Bryene, trans. M.K. Dale, ed. V.B. Redstone (Suffolk Institute of Archaeology and History, 1984).

The Household Books of John Howard, Duke of Norfolk, 1462–1471, 1481–1483, ed. A. Crawford (Stroud, 1992).

Household Books of John, Duke of Norfolk, and Thomas, Earl of Surrey 1481–1490, ed. J.P.Collier (Roxburghe Club, 1844).

Ingulph's *Chronicle of the Abbey of Croyland*, trans. H.T. Riley (1854).

John Leland, *De Rebus Britannicis Collectanea*, ed. T. Hearne, 6 vols (Oxford, 1770).

Dominic Mancini, *The Usurpation of Richard III*, trans. C.A.J. Armstrong (Oxford, 1969, reprinted Gloucester, 1984).

Materials for a History of the Reign of Henry VII, ed. W. Campbell, 2 vols (1873–77).

The Memoirs of Philip de Commines, ed. A.R. Scoble, 2 vols (1856).

More's History of King Richard III, ed. J.R. Lumby (Cambridge, 1883).

St Thomas More, *The History of King Richard III*, ed. R.S. Sylvester (1976).

The Parliament Rolls of Medieval England, ed. C. Given-Wilson *et al* (2005).

The Paston Letters A.D. 1422–1509, ed. J. Gairdner, 6 vols. (1904).

Paston Letters and Papers of the Fifteenth Century, ed. N. Davis, 2 vols (Oxford, 1971 & 1976).

The Plumpton Letters and Papers, ed. J. Kirby (Cambridge, 1996).

A Relation, or rather a true account of the Island of England ... about the year 1500, trans. C.A. Sneyd (Camden Society, 1847).

Report on the Manuscripts of the late Reginald Rawdon Hastings of The Manor House, Ashby de la Zouch, Historical Manuscripts Commission, 78, vol. 1 (1928).

Rolls of Parliament, ed. J Strachey & others, 6 vols (1767–77).

John Rous, *The Rous Roll*, with an historical introduction by Charles Ross (Gloucester, 1980).

'The Last Testament and Inventory of John de Veer, thirteenth Earl of Oxford', ed. W.H. St John Hope, *Archaeologia*, lxvi (1915).

A Calendar of Charters and Other Documents Belonging to the Hospital of William Wyggeston at Leicester, ed. A.H. Thompson (Leicester, 1933).

John Warkworth. *A Chronicle of the first Thirteen Years of the Reign of King Edward the Fourth*, ed. J.O. Halliwell (Camden Society, 1939).

York House Books 1461–1490, ed. L.C. Attreed, 2 vols (Stroud, 1991).

Secondary Sources

Bailey, F.A., 'Some Stanley Heraldic Glass from Worden Hall, Lancashire', *Transactions of the Historic Society of Lancashire and Cheshire,* ci for 1949 (Liverpool, 1950).

Baldwin, D., *The Lost Prince. The Survival of Richard of York* (Stroud, 2007).

Baldwin, D., *Stoke Field: the Last Battle of the Wars of the Roses* (Barnsley, 2006).

Boardman, A.W., *The Battle of Towton* (Stroud, 1994).

Bennett, H.S., *The Pastons and their England* (Cambridge, 1979).

Bennett, M., *The Battle of Bosworth* (Gloucester, 1985).

Chrimes, S.B., *Henry VII* (1984).

Clay, J.W., *The Extinct and Dormant Peerages of the Northern Counties of England* (1913).

Coss, P., *The Lady in Medieval England* (Stroud, 1998).

Coward, B., *The Stanleys, Lords Stanley and Earls of Derby* (Manchester, 1983).

Crawford, A., 'Victims of attainder; the Howard and de Vere women in the late fifteenth century' in K. Bate and M. Barber, eds, *Medieval Women in Southern England*, Reading Medieval Studies, vol. 15 (1989).

Cunningham, S., *Henry VII* (Abingdon, 2007).

Dunham, W.H., 'Lord Hastings' Indentured Retainers, 1461–1483', *Transactions of the Connecticut Academy of Arts and Sciences*, xxxix (New Haven, 1955).

Fuller, T., *History of the Worthies of England* (1662).

G.E.C. *et al.*, *The Complete Peerage*, 14 vols. (1910–98). 1 (Arundel) 5 (Fitzhugh) 6 (Harrington).

Goodman, A., *The Wars of the Roses: Military Activity and English Society 1452–1497* (1981).

Gray H.L., 'Incomes from Land in England in 1436', *English Historical Review*, 49 (1934).

Griffiths, R.A., *The Reign of Henry VI* (2nd edn, 2004).

Guy, J., *Tudor England* (Oxford, 1990).

Hammond, P.W., *The Battles of Barnet and Tewkesbury* (Gloucester, 1990).

Hammond, P.W., 'The Funeral of Richard Neville, Earl of Salisbury' *The Ricardian*, vi (1984).

Hampton, W.E., *Memorials of the Wars of the Roses. A Biographical Guide* (Upminster, 1979).

Hicks, M., *Warwick the Kingmaker* (Oxford, 1998).

Henry E. Huntington Library. Hastings Manuscripts, ed. K. Watson. HMSO 1987. (List & Index Society Special Series, vol. 22).

Jones M.K., & Underwood, M.G., *The King's Mother* (Cambridge, 1992).

Kendall, P.M., *Warwick the Kingmaker* (1957).

Mackie, J.D., *The Earlier Tudors 1485–1558* (Oxford, 1985).

Majendie, S.A.A., *Some Account of the Family of De Vere, The Earls of Oxford, and of Hedingham Castle in Essex* (1904).

Marks, R., *Gothic: Art for England 1400–1547* (2003).

McFarlane, K.B., *England in the Fifteenth Century* (1981).

McFarlane, K.B., *The Nobility of Later Medieval England* (Oxford, 1973)

Meale, C.M., '"… alle the bokes that I have of latyn, englisch and frensch":

Lay Women and their Books in Late Medieval England', in C.M. Meale (ed.) *Women and Literature in Britain 1150–1500* (Cambridge, 1996).

Mitchell, R.J., *John Tiptoft* (1938).

Nichols, J., *The History and Antiquities of the County of Leicester,* 4 vols. (1795–1811).

Oman, C.W., *Warwick the Kingmaker* (1893).

Orme, N., *Medieval Children* (2001).

Oxford Dictionary of National Biography, ed. H.C.G. Matthew and B. Harrison, 60 vols (Oxford 2004), 4 (Beauchamp), 25 (Hastings), 43 (Northumberland), 52 (Stanley), 54 (Tiptoft), 56 (Vere).

Pollard, A.J. *Warwick the Kingmaker. Politics, Power and Fame* (2007).

Pugh, T.B., 'The Magnates, Knights and Gentry', in *Fifteenth-Century England 1399–1509,* ed. S.B. Chrimes, C.D. Ross & R.A. Griffiths (Manchester, 1972).

Robinson, J.M., 'Fitzalan Chapel, Arundel', *Country Life* (May 1, 2008).

Ross, C., *Edward IV* (1974).

Ross, C., *Richard III* (1981).

Routh, P., 'Richard Nevile, Earl of Salisbury: The Burghfield Effigy', *The Ricardian,* vi (1984).

Scofield, C.L., 'The early life of John de Vere, earl of Oxford', *English Historical Review,* xxxix (1914).

Sutton, A.F., and Visser-Fuchs, L., with P.W. Hammond. *The Reburial of Richard, Duke of York 21–30 July 1476* (1996).

Swabey, F., *Medieval Gentlewoman. Life in a Gentry Household in the Later Middle Ages* (Stroud, 1999).

Tudor-Craig, P., *Richard III* (National Portrait Gallery Exhibition Catalogue, 1973).

Ward, J.C., *English Noblewomen in the Later Middle Ages* (1992).

Williams, D., 'The hastily drawn up will of William Catesby, esquire, 25 August 1485', *Transactions of the Leicestershire Archaeological and Historical Society,* li (1975–6).

Woolgar, C.M., *The Great Household in Medieval England* (1999).

Wroe, A., *Perkin: A Story of Deception* (2004).

INDEX